Recipes from a Down East Inn

Recipes
from a
Down East Inn

·

Mark Hodesh, Margaret Parker & Katherine Gould

ILLUSTRATIONS BY MARGARET PARKER

Country Roads Press
CASTINE · MAINE

Recipes from a Down East Inn
© 1995 by Mark Hodesh, Margaret Parker, Katherine Gould. All rights reserved.

Published by Country Roads Press
P.O. Box 286, Lower Main Street
Castine, Maine 04421

Text and cover design by Amy Fischer, Camden, Maine.
Cover photographs by Tom Stewart.
Food styling by Cheryl Roberts.
Illustrations by Margaret Parker.
Typesetting by Typeworks, Belfast, Maine.

ISBN 1-56626-114-7

Library of Congress Cataloging-in-Publication Data

Hodesh, Mark.
    Recipes from a Down East inn / Mark Hodesh, Margaret Parker, Katherine Gould.
        p.   cm.
    Includes index.
    ISBN 1-56626-114-7 : $12.95
    1. Cookery, American—New England style. 2. Cookery—Maine. 3. Menus.
4. Castine Inn (Castine, Me.)   I. Parker, Margaret, 1947– . II. Gould, Katherine F.
III. Title.
TX715.2.N48H63   1995
641.5974—dc20   94-5413
                                                                         CIP

We dedicate this book to the town of Castine
whose history, beauty, and serenity attract our summer visitors,
and to its people
who have become our neighbors, our friends,
and our most loyal supporters.

CONTENTS

*I*NTRODUCTION

When people come to the Castine Inn for dinner, they're offered much more than the food and the recipes. The season of the year, the nearly 100-year-old building, the historic village of Castine, the peace of a quiet night's sleep, the dazzling light and water of Penobscot Bay, and the grace of Maine people all add up to a remarkable experience.

What follows is an examination of a season at the Inn from opening day in early May through closing at the end of October. Each chapter centers around an event, like the Fourth of July or the Camden/Castine Yacht Race, and includes the menu for a meal that captures its essence. The reader gets to peek into the inner workings of a busy summer hotel, from a stroll through the garden in June to a wedding party for 100 in August. The Inn sits in the middle of tiny Castine and is intertwined with history that predates the Revolutionary War. The food gives a taste of all these many facets.

We, Mark and Margaret, came from the Midwest by way of New York City. Our daughter Jeanne was born in 1984, the year we bought the Inn. Kathy, who joined us in 1987 from Washington, D.C., is originally from Wyoming.

When we found the three-story summer hotel, built at the turn of the century, it had endured a long period of neglect from a succession of owners. But we saw in it an old commercial building whose original purpose was still viable. Our goal was not a strict historic re-creation but an effort to follow a simple formula: offer the substantial meals and food service appropriate to the legacy of a summer hotel.

As the business grows, every detail that is added, every new recipe that is used, must fit the original concept. It is this consistency that attracts the same kind of people who came to the original establishment, for the same reasons. Now the Inn is as busy as it was in its heyday. Even the crew is made up of the same kind of hardworking people who looked after the guests nearly a century ago. For all of us, this continuity that links the present with the past is a comfort in the modern world.

First
Comes
Breakfast

❖

From the outside, the Inn appears to hibernate all winter, but inside it's a different story, with major construction and repair under way. With the melting snow, carpenters and painters pack up their tools and leave us to unstack the dining room furniture, roll out the oriental rugs, and put winter behind us. By opening day the Inn is warming up to its working rhythm.

A little after five on the first morning, Mark heads for the kitchen, listening for the familiar whir of each compressor and fan. The milkman rolls in with the first delivery, followed by the egg man. As the aroma of the first pot of coffee floats upstairs, the chopping of onions and grating of potatoes pick up the beat. The voices of the morning crew chime in, catching up on winter gossip as they set up for the first breakfast. Now the Inn is running.

At the old summer hotels every meal was substantial and included in the room rate. Our breakfasts follow this tradition. Fresh-squeezed orange juice or prunes stewed with bits of lemon make a fitting start. We are always surprised at how vocal the prune lobby is. It's not that they complain if they don't get their prunes; it's that they're so enthusiastic when they do.

Mark's love for cooking breakfast began with the Fleetwood Diner, his first business, in Ann Arbor, Michigan. There he developed his recipe for corned beef hash. Remarkably, each year some Inn guest recognizes the Fleetwood hash and perfectly poached egg that were the diner's trademark.

Maine's tiny wild blueberries have a more concentrated flavor than their cultivated cousins, and they make great jam. Our blueberry jam is loaded with whole berries and a hint of ginger and citrus. Cheryl, our jam maker, puts up hundreds of jars in our kitchen each season for our own use and for sale. Guests even leave Christmas lists for boxes of jam that we ship out in December.

 STEWED PRUNES WITH LEMON

SERVES 8

Nothing could be easier than stewing prunes. The perfect stewed prune has a tender yet not gooey skin that offers a hint of resistance when chewed. Bits of lemon act as counterpoint to the syrupy sweetness that develops as the prunes cool.

1 12-ounce box dried prunes
2 lemon rings cut into small wedges (including rind)

2 tablespoons sugar

Place all ingredients in a nonreactive saucepan and add just enough cold water to cover. Boil uncovered for 3 minutes. Cool and refrigerate in a stainless steel or plastic container. They will keep for several weeks.

CORNED BEEF HASH WITH A POACHED EGG

SERVES 6

3 medium baking or russet potatoes (not peeled)
10 ounces cooked corned beef (Use leftovers or prepare as for New England Boiled Dinner, page 102)

1 medium Spanish onion
2 tablespoons unsalted butter
6 large eggs, at room temperature

Place potatoes in heavily salted cold water. Simmer for about 20 minutes, until potatoes just slowly slip off the blade of a paring knife plunged halfway into them. Drain and refrigerate uncovered overnight. (If you don't let the potatoes cool thoroughly, you will end up with a gooey, starchy mess rather than light, separate shreds.) Shred the potatoes on a coarse hand grater.

Slice the corned beef against the grain into ⅛-inch-thick slices and chop into rough pieces.

Dice the onion and sauté in butter until limp.

In a large bowl, combine the potatoes, onions, and corned beef. Toss together lightly; never squeeze, never crush with a spoon. Season to taste with black pepper.

Cook in a large, lightly oiled iron skillet over medium-high heat until brown and crisp on both sides. Serve with a poached egg on top.

Mostly it takes practice to poach a perfect egg, but other key elements are fresh eggs at room temperature and simmering, not boiling, water. The egg white should adhere to and protect the yolk from overcooking. If, when dropped into the simmering water, the white floats to all corners of the pan, the egg is not fresh and will not poach satisfactorily.

WILD BLUEBERRY JAM

MAKES 23 8-OUNCE JARS

While commercial blueberry jam may contain a percentage of applesauce, our recipe is all blueberries with just a hint of lemon, orange, and ginger to enhance and brighten their flavor. It is neither tart nor cloyingly sweet.

3 quarts fresh or frozen wild blueberries, if available, or substitute cultivated berries
1 orange
1 lemon

1 ounce fresh ginger, peeled and cut into 1-inch chunks
1¼ cups powdered pectin
2 tablespoons butter
12 cups sugar

Crush berries lightly with the back of a large wooden spoon and place them in a heavy, nonreactive pot. Cut the orange and lemon (rind and all) into chunks, removing seeds. Place in a food processor with the ginger and process until puréed. (We call this paste "jam stuff.") To the berries add the pectin, "jam stuff," and butter. Quickly bring to a boil and cook for 1 minute. Add the sugar and return to a boil for 1 minute. Immediately ladle jam into hot sterilized jars, filling to within ⅛ inch of the top. Wipe rims clean, screw on two-piece canning lids, and process according to manufacturer's instructions.

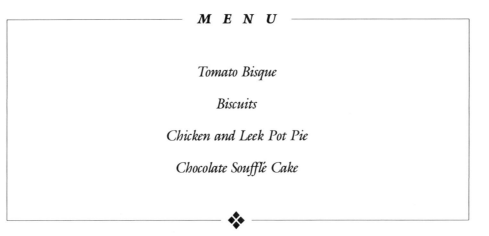

MENU

Tomato Bisque

Biscuits

Chicken and Leek Pot Pie

Chocolate Soufflé Cake

❖

Opening Night

The dining room fills on opening night with friends from town, families of students graduating from the Maine Maritime Academy (just up the hill from us), and visitors eager to unwrap from winter. Warmth and conviviality spread where there is plenty of light to see the food and no background music to muddle thoughts and conversation. Soon the room seems like one big party, with strangers calling from table to table. Castine is a tiny peninsula, almost an island, and this intimacy is contagious. In 1989 Margaret painted a mural that wraps around the dining room. It depicts the Castine peninsula as it surrounds the Inn, from the town dock to the open waters of Penobscot Bay, the stately town common to the wild salt marsh of Hatch's Cove.

This little peninsula played a pivotal role in the earliest battles for the American continent. It is strategically nestled on Penobscot Bay where the waters of the Penobscot and Bagaduce Rivers converge. The battlements of three forts remain from the Revolutionary War and the War of 1812. The British once hoped to move the boundary of Canada south to the Penobscot River, using Castine as their stronghold. They went so far as to dig a canal across ''the neck'' to cut off the peninsula completely from the mainland. The British Canal still gleams like a thin snake through the salt marsh flats.

We cook at the Inn with a simple goal in mind: to make traditional dishes a delicious surprise. Tomato bisque, for example, may have been relegated to the commonplace, yet when well prepared with dill and caraway it is extraordinary. Biscuits are homey and served right from their baking tin. Batch after batch goes into the oven and out to the dining room all night, so they are always hot, light, and fresh. Meat pies were a staple of English cookery. Our recipe for chicken and leek pot pie evolved from a contribution of Mark's mother, Annette Churchill Hodesh. It blends the flavors of chicken, leeks, and fresh tarragon through several stages of cooking. Crowned with a puff pastry crust, it has become one of our most requested meals. The airy chocolate cake, made with no flour at all, is actually a soufflé. Sprinkled with powdered sugar and a white cap of softly whipped cream, it brings opening night to a memorable conclusion.

TOMATO BISQUE

SERVES 8 AS A FIRST COURSE

At the times of year when fresh ingredients are scarce, this soup adds a welcome dimension to the menu, because it is delicious made with canned tomatoes.

1 medium onion, diced
¼ cup unsalted butter
1 teaspoon dill seed
1 tablespoon fresh dill weed
1½ teaspoons dried oregano
1 tablespoon caraway seed
2 tablespoons flour and 2 tablespoons butter cooked as a roux
4 cups chicken stock (2 13¾-ounce cans are close enough)
5 cups fresh tomatoes, diced, or 3 28-ounce cans, drained and chopped

2 medium carrots, peeled and shredded on a hand grater
2 teaspoons salt or to taste (less if using canned chicken stock or bouillon cubes)
½ teaspoon freshly ground black pepper
2 tablespoons honey
¼ cup chopped Italian (flat-leaf) parsley (or substitute curly parsley)
1½ cups heavy cream (not ultra-pasteurized)*
Sour cream and chopped chives for garnish

Sauté the onion in butter until translucent, but do not brown. Add herbs and continue to sauté for a minute or so (this intensifies the flavor of the herbs and improves the soup immensely). Add the roux and stir. Add the stock, tomatoes, and carrots and simmer for 25 minutes. Add the salt, pepper, and honey and put through a food mill. Some of the pulp should come through to lend body to the soup. Finish the soup by adding the parsley and cream and checking again for salt and pepper. Sour cream and chopped chives make a nice garnish.

*We don't like the taste or cooking properties of ultra-pasteurized milk products. When heavy cream is called for, we mean pasteurized only.

BISCUITS

MAKES 18

These biscuits are the cornerstone of our culinary identity, and the recipe is our most often requested one. They are light and crumbly, mottled tan and brown, and they take to buttering. They are a cross between a drop biscuit and a rolled and cut biscuit. Substitute heavy cream for the buttermilk, and they are excellent for strawberry shortcake, too.

4½ cups cake flour (preferably Softasilk)
1½ teaspoons salt
¼ cup sugar
¼ teaspoon nutmeg
2½ tablespoons baking powder

1 cup vegetable shortening
1 cup buttermilk
2 eggs
7 tablespoons water

EGG WASH

1 egg

2 tablespoons milk

Sift dry ingredients together in a large bowl. Cut in the shortening using a pastry blender or working lightly with your fingers. In a separate bowl, whisk the eggs and stir in the buttermilk and water. Make a well in the dry ingredients and add liquid all at once. Work lightly by hand with a fluffing motion until dry ingredients are just moist. Don't overwork. Turn out on a floured surface and spread gently to 1½ inches thick. (When combining dry and wet ingredients, and when spreading the dough, remember that it's the air in the dough that makes the biscuits light. Never knead, overwork, or compress, as this removes the air.) Cut with a 2-inch biscuit cutter and place on an ungreased baking pan. Beat together the egg and the milk and brush the biscuit tops lightly. Bake at 400° for 15 to 18 minutes, or until nicely browned.

CHICKEN AND LEEK POT PIE

SERVES 6

Most people associate chicken pot pie with the frozen food aisle of the supermarket or see it as a vehicle for leftovers. When Mark ordered a chicken pie at the Coach House in New York years ago, he realized there was a higher standard. Over the years, our version has evolved through contributions from Mark's mother and our own fine-tuning in the Inn kitchen. It is now a delicate, creamy concentration of the flavors of chicken, leeks, carrots, and tarragon.

1 roasting chicken (about 6 pounds)
2 cups chicken stock
½ pound carrots, cut into 1-inch sticks
2 large leeks, split, washed, and chopped
2 tablespoon chopped fresh tarragon
½ cup white wine
2 cups cream
Roux made of ½ cup flour cooked with
   6 tablespoons unsalted butter

½ teaspoon Tabasco sauce
½ teaspoon ground thyme
½ teaspoon white pepper
1 teaspoon salt or to taste (less if using
   canned chicken stock)
2 10″ x 10″ sheets of frozen puff pastry
1 egg
2 tablespoons milk

Split the chicken across the stomach cavity and break its back so that the legs are separated from the breast and wings. Bring 4 quarts water to a simmer, add the leg portion, and poach for 25 minutes. Add the breast and continue poaching for another 25 minutes. The chicken should just be cooked through. Remove from broth, cool, pick and cube the meat, and set aside. (If you are making your own chicken stock, return the bones to the broth; discard skin, fat, and cartilage.)

In 2 cups chicken stock simmer the carrots until just tender, 3 to 5 minutes. Remove with a slotted spoon and add to the diced chicken meat; simmer the leeks in the stock until tender, 5 to 6 minutes. Add them to the chicken along with the tarragon.

To the stock, add the wine and simmer to remove the alcohol, about 10 minutes. Add the cream and bring to a boil. Slowly add the roux, stirring, until the desired thickness is reached. (Check the thickening carefully; you may not need all the roux.) Add Tabasco, thyme, salt, and white pepper. Cool the sauce, check for seasoning, pour over the chicken and vegetables, and stir. The pie may be prepared up to this point a day ahead of time.

Divide the mixture among 6 individual, ungreased casserole dishes. Roll the puff pastry sheets lightly and cut circles just slightly larger than the dishes. Lay the pastry over the tops of the dishes and press around the outside to seal. Whisk egg with 2 tablespoons milk and brush the crusts. Bake for about 15 minutes in a 400° oven, or until the filling is hot and the crusts are puffed and brown.

CHOCOLATE SOUFFLÉ CAKE

SERVES 10

8 ounces semisweet chocolate
8 ounces unsalted butter, melted
2 tablespoons salad oil
8 large eggs, separated

1 cup sugar
1 teaspoon vanilla
¼ teaspoon salt

Butter a 12-cup Bundt pan and sprinkle with granulated sugar.

Melt chocolate in a double boiler until just melted and smooth. Add butter and oil, whisk until smooth, and remove from heat. To the egg yolks, add 1 tablespoon water and stir a bit in a mixing bowl. Add half the chocolate and stir; then add the remaining chocolate and mix. Add the sugar and vanilla.

Add the salt to the egg whites and beat until they hold a firm peak but are not dry. (Beating the egg whites just right is the key to this recipe—too soft and they don't hold the volume they should, too dry and they do not fold properly into the batter.) Fold ⅓ of the egg whites thoroughly into the chocolate mixture; then fold in the rest of the whites gently, until just mixed.

Turn into the pan and bake in the bottom third of a preheated 300° oven for 2¼ hours. (A pan of water in the oven will help prevent the top from cracking as it bakes.) Let cool 5 minutes and turn out on a plate. Cool completely.

Dust with confectioners sugar and serve with whipped cream.

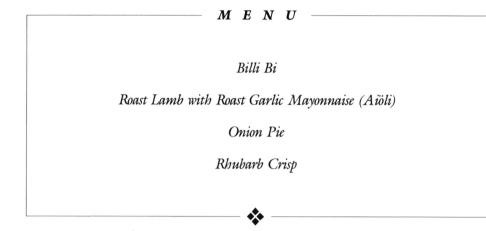

M E N U

Billi Bi

Roast Lamb with Roast Garlic Mayonnaise (Aïoli)

Onion Pie

Rhubarb Crisp

❖

Spring
in
the
Garden

Spring comes late but lasts long in Down East Maine. In the garden beside the Inn, we revel in each new shoot and green leaf as it appears in this unhurried progression. Water seeps from every pore of the rocky peninsula, and runoff rushes down our streambed, soon to be covered with many varieties of iris. Under an overgrown cedar hedge at the edge of the garden, local ferns and dwarf evergreens flourish. Old-fashioned shrub roses mix with aromatic herbs in a profusion of bloom throughout June. A double row of peonies, some from Margaret's mother and grandmother, regally unfold their buds. Meadow flowers such as lupine, monkshood, lythrum, and black-eyed susans burst out in careless waves all summer long.

The garden was planned by Margaret in 1987 as a public place, not just for Inn guests but for all to enjoy. The broad side of the Inn makes a commanding backdrop for the garden. Its Italianate details and long piazza call for a formal design. A massive dry rock wall separates the garden from distractions. Margaret's parents, Gilbert and Pauline Parker, lent invaluable planting experience to the project. Gilbert also built benches, arbors, and the little arched bridge, Jeanne's favorite place. Like classical Italian gardens designed to be seen from above, the formal layout is most distinctive when seen from the second- and third-floor guest rooms. From the piazza, one looks over the rock wall through trees and flowers to the sea.

As the garden matures each year it becomes a more vital extension of the Inn. Visitors spend hours wandering from plant to plant or simply dreaming in the sun. A profusion of cutting flowers brings the peak of each season into the Inn.

Springtime appetites crave fresh young shoots and tender morsels, and the Inn's kitchen responds. Billi Bi has been called one of the world's great soups. It is a creamy bisque made from the liquor of steamed mussels, a prolific Maine shellfish. (We save the silvery blue-gray shells to decorate the knot garden.) Roast lamb served with fresh asparagus tips is a spring delicacy. A slice of onion pie, from a recipe given us by our neighbor Muriel Catuna, makes a distinctive side dish. When the huge leaves of rhubarb unfurl to their tropical proportions, traditional dessert satisfies a long winter's hunger for the tartness of fruit.

ℬILLI BI (Mussel Bisque)

SERVES 8

3 pounds mussels in their shells
1 quart mussel broth (from steaming the
  mussels)
1 pint heavy cream (not ultra-pasteurized)
½ cup dry white wine

Roux of ⅓ cup butter cooked with ⅓ cup
  flour
White pepper to taste (Salt is rarely needed
  as the mussels are naturally salty)
Chopped chives

Scrub the mussels well under cold running water and debeard. Discard any that have cracked or broken shells or that don't close when handled. Steam for about 5 minutes in a covered pot with 4 cups of water. Remove the mussels from the broth and discard any that have not opened. Shuck the mussels and set the meats aside.

Strain the broth through several layers of cheesecloth to remove any sand. Bring 1 quart of the broth to a boil in a nonreactive pot. Add the cream and wine and simmer for 20 minutes. Add the roux and simmer 10 minutes longer. (Be careful; simmering longer will reduce the liquid and make the soup too salty.) Season with white pepper to taste. Return the mussel meats to the soup to reheat. Garnish each bowl with chopped chives.

LEG OF LAMB WITH ROAST GARLIC MAYONNAISE (Aiöli)

SERVES 8

We serve our lamb very rare and garlicky. If you prefer yours with a little less garlic, omit the slivers in the meat or serve the lamb with pan juices (made by deglazing the roasting pan) rather than with the garlic mayonnaise. Serve with fresh asparagus tips.

1 whole leg of lamb, boned, rolled, and tied (5 to 6 pounds)
Slivered garlic
5 garlic cloves, minced
1 teaspoon fresh thyme, preferably French
Zest of 1 lemon
Juice of ½ lemon
1 teaspoon salt
½ teaspoon freshly ground black pepper
1 tablespoon unsalted butter, softened

The day before you plan to roast the lamb, remove it from its plastic wrapping and refrigerate, loosely covered, allowing the meat to "breathe" overnight. About 2 hours ahead of roasting time, remove the meat from the refrigerator, make incisions every inch or so in the top of the roast with the sharp point of a knife, and insert slivers of garlic. Chop together the garlic, thyme, and lemon zest. Stir in lemon juice and other seasonings and mix with the butter. Rub the outside of the meat thoroughly with the herb butter. (If you are boning the meat yourself, also rub the inside of the meat with this mixture before rolling and tying.)

Roast the meat uncovered in a 450° oven until you hear it sizzle, about 15 minutes. Reduce the temperature to 350° and continue roasting until the meat's internal temperature is 125° to 130°, about 1 hour and 15 minutes. Allow the meat to rest 15 minutes before slicing.

We like to carve the lamb into thin slices—3 to 4 per person—and drizzle each serving with a little roast garlic mayonnaise (aiöli). See page 69 for the recipe.

ONION PIE

SERVES 8

6 slices lean bacon, cooked crisp
6 medium onions, thinly sliced
1 tablespoon unsalted butter
1 tablespoon flour
1 cup sour cream
4 large eggs

Salt and pepper to taste
Pinch of nutmeg
One 9-inch unbaked pie shell (Brush the shell with a little beaten egg white if you want. It helps keep the crust from becoming soggy.)

Sauté onions and crumbled bacon with the butter until slightly soft. Sprinkle the flour in and cook for 1 minute; add the sour cream and mix to incorporate. Off heat, mix in the eggs one at a time. Season with salt, pepper, and nutmeg. Stir once more and pour into pie shell. Bake at 350° for 30 to 35 minutes, until the filling is set and the top is brown.

RHUBARB CRISP

SERVES 6

1½ pounds trimmed rhubarb stalks
¾ cup sugar
2 tablespoons flour

Grated zest of ½ lemon
¼ teaspoon nutmeg

Cut rhubarb into ¾-inch pieces. Toss with remaining ingredients and let stand for 15 minutes.

TOPPING

¾ cup flour
½ cup dark brown sugar

6 tablespoons unsalted butter, slightly softened

Mix the flour and sugar to combine, then cut in the butter with a fork or work with your fingers until fine. (Don't use a food processor.)

Put the rhubarb mixture in an 8" x 8" ungreased baking dish and cover generously with topping. Do not press down. Bake at 375° for 40 minutes, or until the fruit is tender and the topping has melted into it. Serve warm with heavy cream, English sauce, or vanilla ice cream.

ENGLISH SAUCE

2 cups milk
4 egg yolks
¼ cup sugar

½ teaspoon vanilla
1 tablespoon triple sec

Bring the milk to a boil in a heavy-bottomed stainless steel saucepan. Remove from heat and cool slightly. In a bowl, whisk the yolks lightly with a splash of water. Whisk the milk slowly into the yolks, being careful to warm the yolks gradually and not scramble them. Return the mixture to the heavy pan; add the sugar, vanilla, and triple sec. Cook slowly, stirring constantly, until the mixture thickens. Strain through a fine sieve into a chilled bowl. The sauce will continue to thicken as it cools.

MENU

Mixed Green Salad with Sherry Vinaigrette

Broiled Salmon with Lemon-and-Egg Sauce

Boiled New Potatoes

Strawberry Shortcake

❖

Fourth
of
July

❖

The Fourth of July heralds the beginning of the "summer season," just as it did a hundred years ago, when families first began to migrate from the hot and grimy cities for entire summers. From all along the eastern seaboard and into the Midwest, people traveled for days by train, then took steamers up the coast, heading for tiny villages almost inaccessible by road. Ladies in hoop skirts, children, pets, and servants were unloaded at the town dock, intent upon a summer of rusticating. This was the era for which the Castine Inn was built, in 1898. Then it had a flat roof for promenades, a second-floor balcony overlooking the street, and a piazza the length of the first floor—a place to see and be seen. Though much has changed in summer travel and at the Inn, Maine still offers a simple but elegant summer respite from the city.

Now, as then, the Fourth of July begins when the whole town turns out on the Common for the parade. In Castine that means lots of kids in costumes or riding decorated bicycles. It's not a long parade, just up the block and back, but what it lacks in length it makes up in fun. There are prizes for all, then three-legged sack races, ferocious tugs-of-war, and rides on fire engines that circle the town, draped with kids, sirens wailing. At dark, fireworks over the harbor give a final salute to Independence Day.

In the lull between revelries, thoughts turn toward dinner. "The ONLY meal for the Fourth of July," a doyenne of earlier days stated emphatically, "is fresh salmon, garden peas, new Maine potatoes, and strawberry shortcake." A 1907 menu from Castine's grandest summer hotel, the 100-room Acadia, offered egg sauce with its salmon. We serve a variation of that traditional New England sauce.

This traditional menu celebrates the beginning of the season, when all these ingredients are available locally. Nothing beats crisp peas and tiny new potatoes, harvested fresh from the Dennis King Farm in Penobscot. A 12-pound salmon, only hours out of the water, is a triumph stretched out on the butcher block. With a few hot days in July, local strawberries ripen to an irresistible sweetness. When these long-awaited favorites converge in one meal, bring on the parades, sirens, and fireworks and let summer begin!

$\mathscr{M}$IXED GREEN SALAD WITH SHERRY VINAIGRETTE

SERVES 6

We serve a simple salad using several different greens, according to what is available. Red and green leaf, oakleaf, and Boston lettuce are our favorites.

2 medium heads leaf lettuce
1 Belgian endive
4 radishes, sliced thin

12 cherry tomatoes, halved
Freshly ground pepper

Thoroughly rinse the lettuce; tear the leaves into bite-sized pieces, then rinse again. Spin in a salad spinner until very dry. The secret to a fresh, crisp salad lies in removing all the water from the greens. We refrigerate lettuce over the evening in a container covered with a damp cloth.

At serving time, toss lightly with vinaigrette until leaves are slightly moist, using about ¼ cup dressing. Garnish with slivers of Belgian endive, sliced radish and cherry tomato. Season with freshly ground pepper.

SHERRY VINAIGRETTE   (Makes 2½ cups)

½ cup sherry vinegar
2 cups olive oil
1 clove garlic, crushed

2 teaspoons Dijon mustard
Salt and pepper to taste

Whisk all ingredients together. Check again for salt and pepper before using. This dressing may be kept for weeks in the refrigerator, but remember to remove the garlic after several days.

BROILED SALMON WITH LEMON-AND-EGG SAUCE

SERVES 6

Fish, properly stored, retains its flavor and character for three days after it is caught. It may not spoil if kept up to a week, but the quality of the flavor and texture drops off markedly after the third day. The problem with picking out a nice piece of fish at the grocery store or fish market is that the standard tests for freshness (red gills, firm flesh, sweet odor) are easiest to discern in whole fish. Once a fish is butchered and iced or wrapped, the best chance of getting something fresh depends on your rapport with the seller. Be nice to your fishmonger, and be sure to ask questions.

6 salmon fillets, about 7 ounces each

Preheat the broiler. Brush both sides of the fillets lightly with vegetable oil and place about 4 inches under the broiler, skin side down, for 5 to 6 minutes. Brush the fillets with melted butter, season with salt and pepper, and continue broiling for a minute or two. To test for doneness: the flesh should feel just firm to the touch, and flakes should separate easily. Flesh should be opaque rather than translucent, but beware of overcooking. Remember that the fish will continue to cook after it is removed from the heat. A slightly underdone piece of fish is far better than one that has been dried out by overcooking. Spoon Lemon-and-Egg Sauce over the center of each fillet and serve immediately.

LEMON-AND-EGG SAUCE

This traditional New England sauce for fish is a country cousin of hollandaise.

4 scallions, minced
½ cup white wine
1 cup heavy cream (not ultra-pasteurized)
1 cup unsalted butter, cut into pieces, room temperature

Juice of one lemon
Salt and pepper
4 hard-boiled eggs, chopped
¼ cup chopped parsley

Place the scallions and wine in a small, heavy enamel or stainless steel saucepan and reduce gently until nearly dry. Add the cream and reduce by about one-third, until thick. Off heat, whisk in the butter gradually. Strain the sauce through a fine sieve and add lemon juice, salt, and pepper to taste. Add the chopped eggs and parsley. Keep the sauce warm over very low indirect heat. Do not boil again or the sauce will break.

BOILED NEW POTATOES

SERVES 6

To us, attention to detail is what makes a meal memorable. If the potato is less than

2 pounds new potatoes, red or white
4 tablespoons butter, at room temperature
2 tablespoons Italian (flat-leaf) parsley,
  chopped

D on't plop one lonely spud in a pot of water, boil the bejesus out of it, and expect it to taste any different from boiled water. New potatoes' tender skins add to their flavor, so there is no need to peel them. Choose potatoes of uniform size, or cut them to size. Barely cover with cold water, add more salt than you think is wise, and bring to a simmer. The potatoes are done when they just slide off the point of a thin knife. Drain immediately, cool slightly, and toss with

excellent, the perfect fish that accompanies it cannot soar.

Salt and pepper to taste

room-temperature butter (cold butter will break when added to hot potatoes). Add salt, pepper, and chopped Italian (flat-leaf) parsley. Fresh dill is a nice alternative.

Should you need to hold the potatoes for half an hour or so before serving (as we often do at the Inn), cover them loosely with a cloth that allows them to breathe. A tight lid will trap steam that continues the cooking.

STRAWBERRY SHORTCAKE

SERVES 6 TO 8

1 quart strawberries
¾ ounce triple sec
¼ cup sugar (or more if berries are very tart)

Grenadine (optional)

Clean and hull the berries. Purée half of them in a food processor with the triple sec and the sugar. A little grenadine can be added here for color, not flavor. Slice the remaining berries and mix into the purée. This sauce is best if refrigerated overnight but served at room temperature.

SHORTCAKE BISCUITS (Makes 10)

1 tablespoon sugar
2 cups flour
1 tablespoon baking powder
1 teaspoon salt

¼ cup unsalted butter, cut into pieces and frozen
1 cup plus 2 tablespoons heavy cream

Sift dry ingredients together. Cut in the butter with a fork or pastry blender until crumbly and pebbly. Add the cream and mix until just combined. Turn out onto a floured surface, handling only enough to make a cohesive dough, and roll ¾-inch thick. Cut biscuits with a 3-inch cutter, brush their tops with milk, and sprinkle lightly with granulated sugar. Arrange on ungreased baking sheet and bake at 425° for 8 to 10 minutes, or until light brown.

To serve: Split the warm biscuits in half and dust the tops with confectioners sugar. Put the biscuit bottom on a dessert plate and spoon sauce over it. Add a dollop of softly whipped cream and replace the biscuit top.

MENU

White Bean Salad with Vinaigrette

Pasta Salad

Marinated Bean and Walnut Salad

Poached Salmon with Remoulade Sauce

◆

Prime Rib with Horseradish Sauce

Roast Chicken

Seafood Stew

◆

Tapioca Pudding with Apricot Sauce

Cheesecake with Blueberry Sauce

Chocolate Walnut Brownies

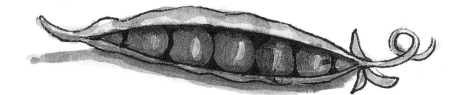

Tuesday
Night
Buffet

❖

Castine came into its prime after the War of 1812. It grew from a trading and military outpost to become the shire town of Hancock County, hosting the county courts. Its central location by water made it the hub of activity for miles around. The harbor bristled with the masts of ships that plied trade routes along the coast, to the West Indies and beyond. A wealth of timber for ships' hulls and spars grew close at hand, keeping local shipyards busy building the great wooden sailing vessels of the era. The village bustled with trade in timber, ice, bricks, salt, and lime. Sail lofts, ships chandleries, blacksmith shops, and general stores thrived. Sea captains, merchants, and lumber barons began building the large homes that line Main Street even today. Though the courts moved away in 1838 and shipping turned from sails to steam in the 1870s, early prosperity left its indelible stamp on the town.

People come to Castine today for a completely different reason—to find the peace and quiet of an historic village. But on Tuesday nights something happens that would make those industrious merchants and traders of old take notice. Cars line both sides of Main Street, and friends in shirts sleeves or their Sunday best rub elbows at the Castine Inn. The Tuesday Night Buffet is an evening as sociable as a church supper, with a choice of dishes that are subtly complementary. A guest entering the dining room is greeted with a table laden with salads—glistening pasta flecked with tomatoes, marinated beets and walnuts, and a white bean salad—surrounding a regal poached salmon. A server stands ready to carve a slice of rare prime rib or roast chicken, or to dish up an aromatic seafood stew. Somehow room is found on the plate for steamed vegetables and crunchy roasted potatoes, but diners' hopes of coming back for seconds fade in front of the dessert table. Choosing among tapioca pudding topped with apricot sauce, creamy wedges of cheesecake, stacks of dark chocolate brownies, and a colorful mountain of freshly cut fruit would be difficult, but small portions make it possible to sample them all.

The abundance of delicious choices to mix to one's choosing, the navigation of full plates back to the table at one's own rate, and neighborly conversations while lined up for more have made the Tuesday Night Buffet a port of call not to be missed.

WHITE BEAN SALAD WITH VINAIGRETTE

SERVES 8 TO 10

Success with this salad depends on getting the beans cooked just right. Cooked too long, they turn to mush; cooked too little, they will be crunchy when they cool.

1 pound white beans, soaked overnight
4 cloves garlic, minced
1 red onion, finely chopped

¼ cup chopped fresh tarragon
2 tablespoons chopped fresh mint leaves
Salt and pepper to taste

Drain the beans and rinse them. Cover with cold water by 2 inches and simmer up to 2 hours, until the beans are very soft but have not burst. Drain and toss with vinaigrette while still warm. Cool to room temperature and add the garlic, onion, tarragon, mint, salt, and pepper.

VINAIGRETTE

½ cup sherry vinegar
1 tablespoon Dijon mustard

1 teaspoon sugar
⅔ cup olive oil

Mix vinegar, mustard, and sugar in a food processor. With the motor running, add the oil in a slow, steady stream until incorporated.

PASTA SALAD
SERVES 6 TO 8

Our pasta salad is a simple one—vegetables, herbs, and vinaigrette dressing tossed with pasta. Variations are unlimited, and we often add a little something extra depending on what's available, maybe black olives, green onions, capers, or sun-dried tomatoes.

2 medium tomatoes, scalded, skinned, seeded, chopped, and drained
1 cup chopped red or green pepper
½ red onion, diced
1 teaspoon minced garlic
½ cup finely chopped fresh basil
1 tablespoon salt and ¾ teaspoon fresh-ground black pepper, or to taste

½ cup strong vinaigrette made with ⅙ cup vinegar and ⅓ cup olive oil (hazelnut oil may be substituted for part of the olive oil)
1 pound good-quality pasta in a sturdy shape, such as *ziti* or *penne rigate*
Imported parmesan cheese, freshly grated

Combine the vegetables, herbs, seasonings, and vinaigrette in a large nonreactive bowl. Cook the pasta until barely done in 5 quarts rapidly boiling, heavily salted water to which a little oil has been added. When done, drain the pasta and immediately toss it with the vegetables, herbs, seasonings, and dressing. The warm pasta will absorb the vinaigrette as it cools. Chill the salad and sprinkle with parmesan cheese just before serving.

MARINATED BEET AND WALNUT SALAD

SERVES 8 TO 10

10 to 12 medium beets, scrubbed and
   trimmed
Vinaigrette made with equal parts red-
   wine vinegar and walnut (or hazelnut)
   oil, about ¼ cup each

1 cup coarsely chopped walnuts
¼ cup chopped fresh dill
Salt and freshly ground black pepper
   to taste

Boil the beets in heavily salted water until tender, 30 to 40 minutes. Cool and rub with a cloth to remove the skins. Cut the beets into ½-inch chunks and toss with enough of the vinaigrette to just coat the beets. Add the walnuts and dill and toss again. Season with salt and pepper. The beets may be cooked and marinated early in the day; add the walnuts and dill just before serving.

 POACHED SALMON WITH REMOULADE SAUCE

SERVES 8 TO 10

For poaching, the temperature of the cooking liquid should be 180°, considerably lower than a true simmer.

Side of salmon, filleted (about 2 pounds)
3 quarts water
3 cups dry white wine
2 large onions, 3 stalks celery, 3 peeled
   carrots, all chopped

2 teaspoons black peppercorns
3 teaspoons fennel seed
1 teaspoon dry thyme leaves

Combine water, wine, and all seasonings in a stainless steel or enamel pot with low sides (for convenience in getting the fish in and out of the broth). Simmer for 20 minutes. Place the salmon skin side down in the liquid, adding water if necessary to completely cover the fish, and poach gently for 15 to 20 minutes. Remove the fish carefully with a spatula. Cool and serve with remoulade sauce.

REMOULADE SAUCE

Remoulade is like a tartar sauce in that its base is mayonnaise, but it carries the tang of capers and gherkins rather than the sweetness of pickle relish.

1 egg
¾ teaspoon salt
¼ teaspoon paprika
1 tablespoon white wine vinegar
1 tablespoon lemon juice
1 cup vegetable oil

2 tablespoons chopped capers
2 tablespoons chopped gherkins
1 tablespoon green peppercorns in vinegar,
   drained and chopped
2 tablespoons chopped fresh dill

In a food processor combine the egg, salt, paprika, vinegar, lemon juice, and ¼ cup of the oil. With the motor running, add the remaining oil in a slow, steady stream. Stir in the remaining ingredients.

PRIME RIB WITH HORSERADISH SAUCE

SERVES 30

11- to 13-pound boneless beef rib eye
Salt and pepper

Minced garlic

The day before you plan to roast the meat, remove it from its plastic wrapping, rub the outside with a combination of salt, pepper, and minced garlic, and refrigerate loosely covered, letting the roast "breathe" overnight. Take it from the refrigerator about 2 hours before roasting and place in a roasting pan, fat side up.

Roast in a 450° oven until you hear sizzling. Reduce the temperature to 350° and continue roasting until the meat reaches an

internal temperature of 110° (about 1 hour and 45 minutes). Remember that a large roast like this will continue to cook after it is removed from the oven and will reach about 125° (rare) by serving time. Cut off and discard the fatty side flap. Let the meat rest for at least 20 minutes; it will stay warm, loosely covered, for up to an hour. It is not necessary that the meat be served *hot*. We slice the beef thin, giving each person one or two slices on a hot plate. Horseradish sauce makes a nice accompaniment.

HORSERADISH SAUCE

1 cup sour cream
2 to 3 tablespoons horseradish

Juice of ½ lemon
Salt and pepper to taste

Combine all ingredients.

ROAST CHICKEN

SERVES 6 TO 8

We use a 5- or 6-pound roasting chicken, preferably fresh, but a frozen chicken thawed in the refrigerator is fine. The day before you plan to roast the chicken, take it out of its plastic wrapper, rinse it thoroughly in cold running water, pat it dry, and rub the outside with seasoned salt. Refrigerate the chicken loosely covered to allow it to "breathe" overnight.

The next day, place the chicken on a rack in a roasting pan and put it in a 450° oven until it sizzles. Lower the heat to 350° and continue to roast until a thermometer inserted in the thickest part of the thigh registers 190° and the leg joints are loose. A chicken this size will take about 1 hour and 45 minutes. Baste periodically during roasting. Allow the chicken to rest 15 minutes before carving.

One of the best things about roast chicken is the leftovers; and we always make stock with the carcass.

SEASONED SALT

In a food processor combine:
¼ **cup juniper berries**
2 **tablespoons crushed bay leaf**
2 **tablespoons dried thyme leaves**
2 **tablespoons dried rosemary**

2 **tablespoons black peppercorns**
2½ **cups kosher salt**

Process until well combined and add:
2 **tablespoons chopped garlic**

This mixture keeps, refrigerated, for months. It may also be used to season beef roast and pork loin.

SEAFOOD STEW

SERVES 8

1 onion, sliced thin
2 tablespoons butter
5 cloves garlic, crushed with a garlic press
1 quart fish stock (may use clam broth or mussel broth)
½ teaspoon finely chopped saffron
½ pint cream
Roux of ¼ cup butter and ¼ cup flour, cooked together

Salt and pepper to taste (as the seafood is naturally salty, additional salt isn't likely to be needed)
2 pounds mussels, rinsed under cold running water and debearded
1 pound shrimp, peeled
1 pound sea scallops, hinges removed

Sauté the onion in the butter until just translucent but do not brown. Add the garlic and sauté a few more minutes. Add the fish stock and saffron and simmer for 30 minutes. Add the cream and reduce for about 15 minutes. Add the roux and simmer for 10 minutes. Adjust salt and pepper.

In a large, flat-bottomed, low-sided pan, heat the sauce to a simmer. Add the mussels, discarding any that do not close when handled, and simmer for 2 minutes; then add the scallops and cook for an additional 2 minutes. Add the shrimp and cook about 4 more minutes, until the mussels open and the seafood is done. Garnish with chopped parsley. This is good served over rice.

TAPIOCA PUDDING WITH APRICOT SAUCE

SERVES 6

Tapioca pudding is something of an overlooked, old-fashioned favorite.

Follow the directions on the box of quick-cooking tapioca for 6 servings of pudding. The secret to light pudding that is not gluey lies in being patient enough to stir it slowly and constantly for about 15 minutes, watching the heat closely so that it does not scorch. A teaspoon of tart apricot sauce complements tapioca perfectly and makes it into a special dessert.

APRICOT SAUCE (Makes 3 cups)

8 ounces dried apricots
3 cups water

½ cup sugar

Stew apricots in water and sugar for 5 minutes. Purée in a food processor or blender. This sauce keeps at least a month in the refrigerator. It is also good on cheesecake (and hot oatmeal!).

CHEESECAKE WITH BLUEBERRY SAUCE

SERVES 12

CRUST

18 pieces Zwieback toast, crushed into crumbs (about 1½ cups)
2 tablespoons sugar

¼ teaspoon cinnamon
⅓ cup melted unsalted butter or margarine

Mix dry ingredients, then mix in melted butter until all the dry crumbs are saturated. Press onto the bottom and sides of a 9″ springform pan. If you butter the sides of the pan lightly, the crumbs will adhere more easily.

FILLING

2½ pounds cream cheese, at room temperature
1¾ cups sugar
2 tablespoons flour
¼ teaspoon salt

1 teaspoon vanilla extract
Zest of 1 lemon (1 teaspoon)
6 large eggs
½ cup heavy cream

Preheat oven to 475°. Beat cream cheese until fluffy. Add sugar, flour, salt, vanilla, and lemon zest gradually, beating well. Mixture should be smooth. Add eggs, one at a time, beating well between additions. Add the cream and blend well. Pour into prepared pan. Bake for 10 minutes at 475°, then reduce the oven temperature to 225° and bake for 1 hour. To prevent the cake from cracking on the top, place a pan of water on the bottom shelf of the oven while baking and, as soon as you remove the cake from the oven, run a small, sharp knife around the edge to loosen the crust from the side of the pan. Do not take the side of the springform off until the cake is completely cool. Do not remove the bottom of the pan at all. Serve wedges with a spoonful of blueberry sauce over the center of each.

BLUEBERRY SAUCE

2 cups fresh or frozen blueberries
⅓ cup sugar
1 teaspoon cornstarch

½ teaspoon grated lemon zest
Approximately ½ cup additional
blueberries

Combine all ingredients except the last ½ cup of berries in a saucepan. Cook over medium heat, stirring frequently, until mixture thickens and the liquid clears (just 5 minutes or so). Incorporate the additional berries after the sauce has cooled.

CHOCOLATE WALNUT BROWNIES

MAKES 18

5 ounces unsweetened chocolate
⅔ cup unsalted butter
4 large eggs, at room temperature
½ teaspoon salt
2 cups sugar

1 teaspoon vanilla extract
¼ teaspoon almond extract
1 cup all-purpose flour, sifted
1 cup walnut pieces

Preheat oven to 450°. Butter a 9″ x 13″ baking pan, and line the bottom with parchment paper. Butter the paper and dust with flour.

Melt the chocolate and butter over hot water until chocolate is just melted and smooth. Whisk to blend and remove from heat.

In a mixer at medium-high speed, beat the eggs and salt until slightly fluffy. Add the sugar in four parts, at 1-minute intervals, and continue to beat for 15 minutes, until very fluffy. This long beating is important. The batter should be satiny and form ribbons when the beaters are raised. Add the vanilla and almond extracts. On the lowest speed, add the chocolate mixture to the eggs and beat only enough to blend. Still on low speed, add the flour and beat just to blend. With a rubber spatula, gently fold in the nuts.

Spread batter evenly in the prepared pan. Reduce the oven temperature to 400° and bake on the oven's lower shelf for 15 to 17 minutes, until a toothpick comes out clean. Do not overbake. Turn out onto a cooling rack, remove the paper, and cool until brownies can be cut.

M E N U

Lentil and Goat Cheese Salad

Crabmeat Cakes with Mustard Sauce

Poached Peaches with Vanilla Ice Cream and Caramel Sauce

❖

The
Camden/Castine
Yacht
Race

The protected waters of Penobscot Bay have long been a haven for commercial sailing vessels of all shapes and sizes. Today, with its deep waters and ever-present winds, the Bay is a paradise for cruising and racing yachtsmen.

On the last Saturday in July the crack of the starting gun sends scores of boats, from large ocean racers to fast little J boats, out from Camden harbor. They will cross miles of open water, round the tip of Islesboro, and end in Castine harbor on the first leg of this two-day race. It may take all-day playing with variable winds, through fog or dead calm, to finish the course, or glorious winds could speed the fleet over in a matter of hours. Hoisting a huge sail under the tension of a race strains the vessel, the ingenuity of the captain, and teamwork of the crew. Boats, crews, and captains return year after year for the challenge of this race.

Castine harbor rising into view is a welcome sight at the end of the day. Crews of 12 to 20 soon fill our dining room, where the day's trials are cheered from table to table. Racers' appetites are notorious. The marinated lentil salad with a slice of tangy goat cheese combines tastes and textures of great gusto. Often a satisfying meal in itself, tonight this appetizer is just a drop in the bucket. What brings the sailors racing back is the crabmeat cakes. Made with our fine-textured, sweet local crab, the cakes are baked, not fried, and served in a pool of mild mustard sauce.

This recipe originated at Gloucester House, one of New York City's legendary seafood restaurants, run for fifty-seven years by Mr. Edmond Lillys. He had the heightened sensibility of the Greeks (now there was a race of sailors) for why people love to eat seafood. Mark worked for Mr. Lillys at Gloucester House for the first five winters that we owned the Inn, returning each summer to Castine immeasurably enriched. Mr. Lillys understood what it takes to stay the course in the restaurant business.

Around the tables, wind-burned faces begin to droop. A cool, simple dessert is called for. One fresh peach poached until tender, mounded with vanilla ice cream and hot, buttery caramel sauce, will top off this superb repast. Tomorrow the sails will be set to race back to Camden.

LENTIL AND GOAT CHEESE SALAD

SERVES 6

1 small onion
1 carrot
1 small leek (white part only)
2 garlic cloves
2 tablespoons olive oil
½ pound green French lentils

Bouquet garni (1 bay leaf, 4 parsley stems,
 1 tablespoon dry thyme (or a sprig of
 fresh French thyme, if available) and 15
 peppercorns, tied in cheesecloth)
2 tablespoons chopped fresh parsley

Mince the onion, carrot, leek, and garlic. Sauté gently in olive oil. Rinse the lentils, place in saucepan with sautéed vegetables, cover by 1 inch with water, and bring to a simmer. Add bouquet garni. Simmer for about 1 hour, adding water if necessary to keep the lentils covered. Lentils should be tender but not mushy. Remove bouquet garni. The mixture should be "swampy"; drain if there's too much liquid. While still hot, toss with the vinaigrette. Cool to room temperature and toss again with chopped parsley.

VINAIGRETTE

2 teaspoons Dijon mustard
2 tablespoons white wine vinegar

⅓ cup olive oil
Salt and pepper to taste

Put mustard and vinegar in a food processor. With machine running, add the oil slowly until incorporated. Add salt and pepper to taste.

6-inch log of goat cheese
Chopped fresh parsley
Olive oil

Roasted, peeled red pepper strips and
 Greek or Moroccan olives for garnish

Slice a log of goat cheese into ½-inch-thick rounds and roll edges in chopped parsley. Place a mound of lentils in the center of a small plate and top with 2 slices of cheese. Drizzle the cheese lightly with olive oil. Garnish the plate with strips of roasted red pepper and imported black olives.

CRABMEAT CAKES WITH MUSTARD SAUCE

SERVES 8

1 cup finely chopped onion
2 tablespoons butter
⅓ cup minced fresh parsley
5 large eggs, beaten lightly
2 tablespoons ground toasted hazelnuts
1 tablespoon Old Bay seasoning
3 tablespoons milk
2½ cups medium cracker meal (or dry bread crumbs)

2 pounds fresh crabmeat, picked over
1 cup dry bread crumbs
¼ cup (½ stick) unsalted butter, melted, for brushing the crabmeat cakes
Chopped parsley and lemon wedges for garnish

Sauté the onion in butter over moderately low heat, stirring occasionally, until it just turns golden. In a large bowl, combine the onion, parsley, eggs, hazelnuts, Old Bay, and the milk. Stir in the cracker meal, forming a thick batter. Add the crabmeat and toss gently with a wooden spoon.

To form, fill a ⅓ cup measure lightly with the crabmeat mixture, invert the cup, and shake out the cake. Sprinkle with the bread

crumbs. Transfer cakes to a baking sheet and bake in the middle of a preheated 450° oven for 8 minutes. Brush the tops with melted butter and broil under a preheated broiler about 4 inches from the heat for 2 to 3 minutes, or until the cakes are golden.

To serve, pool some mustard sauce on a plate and place two crabmeat cakes on it. Garnish with chopped parsley and a lemon wedge.

MUSTARD SAUCE

⅔ cup dry vermouth
3 tablespoons red wine vinegar
2 shallots, minced
3 black peppercorns
1½ cups white fish stock (or bottled clam juice)

2 cups heavy cream (not ultra-pasteurized)
1 cup Dijon-style mustard
⅔ cup sour cream
Salt and white pepper to taste

In a nonreactive saucepan combine the vermouth, vinegar, shallots, and peppercorns. Bring the mixture to a boil and reduce until the liquid is almost evaporated. Add the stock and boil the mixture until it is reduced by half. Add the heavy cream and boil the mixture until it is reduced by one-third. Remove the pan from the heat and whisk in the mustard and sour cream. Season to taste with salt and white pepper. Strain the sauce through a fine sieve into a bowl and keep it warm, covered. (The mustard sauce will keep, refrigerated, for at least a week. If it separates, whisk to restore).

POACHED PEACHES WITH ICE CREAM AND CARAMEL SAUCE

SERVES 6

This recipe depends on good-quality, almost ripe peaches.

6 peaches
4 quarts water
6 cups sugar
½ vanilla bean

Juice of 1 lemon
¼ teaspoon almond extract
Vanilla ice cream

Bring the water to a rapid boil and shock the peaches in it for about 15 seconds to loosen the skins. Remove the peaches to an ice bath, peel them (reserving the skins), halve, and remove pits.

To the water add the sugar, the vanilla bean (split and scraped), the lemon juice, and the peach skins. Bring to a low boil and return the peaches to the liquid. Poach until they are medium soft, testing with a thin knife. Remove from heat and add the almond extract. Cool, then refrigerate in enough of the strained poaching syrup to cover.

To serve, place a scoop of vanilla ice cream in a dessert bowl and arrange a peach half on either side. Spoon warm caramel sauce over.

CARAMEL SAUCE   (Makes 3½ cups)

This makes more sauce than you will need for the poached peach dessert, but it keeps for weeks in the refrigerator.

2½ cups light brown sugar
1½ cups light corn syrup
⅓ cup unsalted butter
½ teaspoon salt

¼ cup water
2 teaspoons vanilla extract
1 cup heavy cream

In a heavy stainless steel saucepan, stir and heat the brown sugar, corn syrup, butter, salt, and water. Boil covered, without stirring, about 5 minutes, until temperature reaches 235° on a candy thermometer.

Let stand off heat, stirring occasionally, for 5 minutes; then add the vanilla. When cooler yet, though still warm, stir in cream to make a shiny, smooth sauce.

Roasted Eggplant Soup

Lobster Curry with Peach Chutney and Condiments

Lemon Meringue Pie

❖

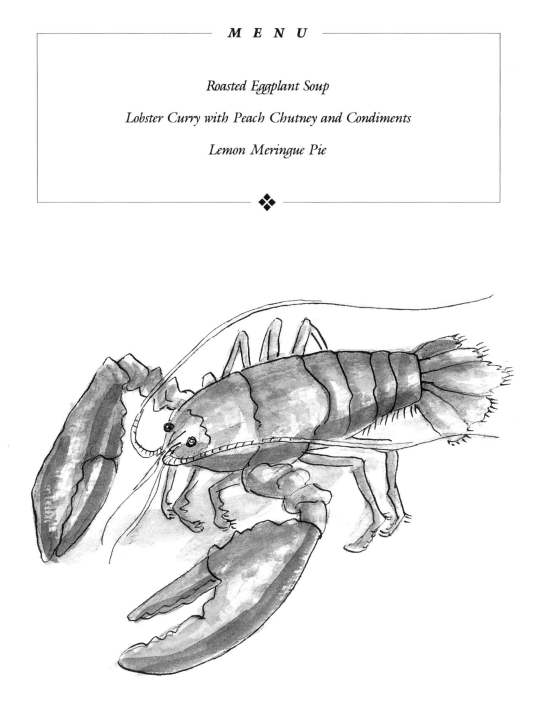

Music
in
the
Garden

❖

The lingering glow of summer evenings is so conducive to music and dancing that three times a summer we set up a band on the Inn's veranda and invite the town to a free concert. The garden becomes a patchwork of picnic blankets and lawn chairs, the driveway makes a dance floor, and the whole Inn hops. Many listeners stay for dinner, filling every table in the dining room, the Churchill Room, the bar, and the prime seats outside near the band.

When we bought the Inn, nothing was left of the "piazza"—as the veranda is known locally—except old photographs. In 1989 we reconstructed it, and its gracious proportions returned the building to its original Italianate design. The building felt whole to us for the first time. Since then, every foot of the Inn has been rejuvenated, from the third-floor guest rooms to the poured concrete basement. On these busy summer nights when the Inn swirls with people and music, we take pride in how smoothly everything runs.

With all our efforts, though, we're constantly reminded that ours is but a short link in the Inn's long history. Years ago a parrot entertained in the bar while the innkeeper was busy rebuilding the roof. Another former owner barricaded himself against the fire marshall to save the building from demolition. Back in the '30s the Inn served as a dormitory for the State Normal School, and alumni still regale us with stories. Then there was the summer the Human Fly scaled the outside wall of the Inn, creating an indelible memory for small boys who witnessed it. And, wonder of wonders, Lucille Ball was once sighted sunbathing on the front porch.

A table on the veranda near the musicians is the place to be on music nights, with the sunset reflecting from islands, clouds, and water. All tastes seem keener in the open air, and the roasted eggplant soup garnished with red pepper cream rises to the occasion. Its robust aroma and subtle earthiness are in delectable syncopation.

A sea captain's wife might have proudly borne back curry spices from the Orient. Our lobster curry is a sumptuous variation on Indian cuisine. The pleasingly hot and intense flavors never overpower the lobster. The counterpoint of peach chutney, grated coconut, and cucumber raita make this a rare feast. With the lightest possible dessert, a slice of lemon meringue pie, one could easily float into the clouds along with the music, the warm breezes, and the afterglow of sunset.

ROASTED EGGPLANT SOUP

SERVES 6

2 medium eggplants
Kosher salt
¼ cup olive oil
Juice of ½ lemon
½ teaspoon ground thyme

12 gloves garlic, unpeeled
4 cups chicken stock
Salt and black pepper to taste
Chopped parsley for garnish

Trim off the stem ends of the eggplants and slice lengthwise into 8 wedges. Place wedges in a colander, salt heavily, and let stand for about 30 minutes. This will remove the bitter juices. Rinse well in cold running water and pat dry with a paper towel.

Place eggplant wedges in a bowl and toss with the olive oil, lemon juice, thyme, and whole garlic cloves. Spread on a baking pan in a single layer, cover with aluminum foil, and bake at 350° for about 35 minutes, or until the eggplant is thoroughly tender.

Pass everything through a medium screen of a food mill. Return the mixture to a saucepan and add 4 cups hot chicken stock. Adjust salt and pepper to taste. Garnish with a dollop of red pepper cream and chopped parsley.

RED PEPPER CREAM

1 red bell pepper

1 cup sour cream

Char the pepper over an open flame or under the broiler. Peel, seed, and purée in a blender. Pass through a strainer and mix with sour cream.

LOBSTER CURRY WITH PEACH CHUTNEY AND CONDIMENTS

SERVES 6

1 onion
4 cloves garlic
1½ ounces fresh ginger
1 pear, peeled and cored
1 apple, peeled and cored
Zest and juice of 1 orange
2 tablespoons vegetable oil
1 teaspoon ground cardamom
½ cinnamon stick, cracked
1 bay leaf
1½ teaspoons ground cumin
1 teaspoon ground coriander
¼ teaspoon (scant) cayenne pepper
½ teaspoon ground turmeric
2 teaspoons hot curry powder
1½ teaspoons sweet curry powder

1 teaspoon salt, or to taste
1 cup lobster stock (or substitute fish stock or bottled clam juice)
¾ cup plain yogurt
1 cup water
1 cup boiled cream
1 tablespoon arrowroot, mixed with ¼ cup cold water
Cooked meat from 6 lobsters, 1½ pounds each
2 ripe tomatoes, peeled, seeded, and chopped
2 cups white rice, preferably Basmati
Fresh cilantro, for garnish
Grated coconut, for accompaniment

Chop the onion, garlic, ginger, pear, and apple and place in a food processor with the orange zest and juice. Process to make a paste.

In a stainless steel saucepan, heat the oil to medium hot, add the cardamom, cinnamon stick, and bay leaf and stir for 20 seconds. Add the paste from the food processor and sauté for 5 minutes. Add the cumin, coriander, cayenne, turmeric, curry powders, and salt, and stir for 1 minute. Add the lobster stock and stir the yogurt in slowly, ¼ cup at a time. Add the water and the cream, and simmer for 10 minutes. Strain through a coarse sieve, pressing the solids. Return to the saucepan and thicken with the arrowroot mixture.

Cook the rice.

Put the whole lobster pieces into the curry sauce just to warm. Add chopped tomato.

Spoon a bed of rice onto each serving plate. Arrange a lobster tail, split or cut into medallions, and two claws over the rice, and spoon on a little extra sauce. Garnish with chopped cilantro. Serve with chutney, grated fresh coconut (or packaged unsweetened coconut), and cucumber raita.

CUCUMBER RAITA

1 large cucumber

1 cup plain yogurt

Peel, seed, and dice cucumber. Mix with yogurt.

PEACH CHUTNEY (Makes 1 quart)

2 pounds firm peaches
½ cup cider vinegar
½ cup dark brown sugar
½ medium onion, chopped
½ pound seedless raisins
2 apples, pared and diced
1½ teaspoons whole mustard seed

**Fresh ginger (a piece as big as your
  thumb), peeled and minced**
1½ teaspoons salt
1½ teaspoons paprika
1½ teaspoons ground cumin
Zest and juice of 1 lemon

Shock peaches in boiling water for about 15 seconds to loosen skin. Peel and slice ¾ inch thick. Place in a nonreactive saucepan, add the vinegar and brown sugar, and set aside. Combine rest of ingredients in another nonreactive saucepan and cook over low heat, stirring constantly until thoroughly blended. Cook peach mixture several minutes, until peaches are tender but still hold their shape. Combine the two mixtures and cook together a few minutes, stirring. (Be careful, it scorches easily.) This makes more than you will need for the lobster curry, but it keeps for a month in the refrigerator and is good with roast pork or chicken.

LEMON MERINGUE PIE

SERVES 8

1 9″ baked pie shell
1 cup sugar
1¾ ounces cornstarch
⅛ teaspoon salt
1 cup cold water

1 cup cold milk
1 ounce unsalted butter
4 eggs, separated
Zest and juice of 2 lemons

In heavy nonreactive saucepan, mix together the sugar, cornstarch, and salt. Add cold water and cold milk, whisk slightly, and stir with a spatula over medium heat until mixture thickens at a boil. Be careful, as it scorches easily at this point. Cook 2 minutes longer. Remove from heat and add butter.

Temper the beaten egg yolks by stirring in a few spoonfuls of the cornstarch mixture; then combine with the remaining mixture. Add lemon juice and zest. Heat to moderate temperature, stirring constantly, for 1 minute.

Allow the filling to cool to lukewarm before turning into the baked pie shell.

MERINGUE

4 egg whites, room temperature
¼ teaspoon cream of tartar

Pinch of salt
½ cup sugar

Combine egg whites, cream of tartar, and salt in a mixing bowl. Beat until the whites barely hold soft peaks. Add the sugar slowly, beating 15 seconds between additions. This is important to getting the maximum volume from the egg whites.

Spread meringue over the filling, being sure to cover evenly, and seal around the edge.

Bake until meringue is lightly colored. This will take 7 to 9 minutes at 325°. Watch carefully to avoid overbrowning.

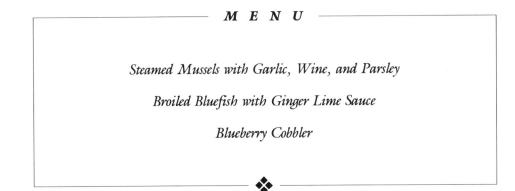

M E N U

Steamed Mussels with Garlic, Wine, and Parsley

Broiled Bluefish with Ginger Lime Sauce

Blueberry Cobbler

Exploring
the
Coast

❖

Many people happen on Castine by chance as they turn off Route 1 to follow the Penobscot River down to the sea. Since the seventeenth century, explorers and colonists have been lured to this peninsula first settled by native peoples, then taken over in turn by the French, the Dutch, the Americans, the British, and the Americans again. From across the Atlantic, Castine was long seen as a foothold on a mighty continent. Today evergreen forests meet saltwater farms, and moose bogs rise into rocky blueberry barrens as Route 175 wanders for 18 miles through the countryside. Just as a traveler's suspicion of being lost takes hold, a quick left turn brings Main Street into full view. Spacious Federal and Victorian houses line both sides of the street in a stately march down the hill to the glittering bay.

Halfway down Main Street on the left sits the Castine Inn. Chance visitors who find the dining room full may slip into the quiet bar, a small room with windows all around and walls as deep green as the sea. The bartender serves an aromatic dish for a customer at the bar, then offers his help. At a corner table, quiet conversation between sailing friends mingles with the irresistible aroma of garlic, wine, and mussels.

Why not stay for dinner, as so many others have done? Soon a cloth is laid, and steaming soup plates of blue-black mussels arrive. The shellfish are extremely tender, and redolent of the briny sea. All around, the tables fill with people displaying obvious anticipation. "Try the local bluefish, it's in season," one neighbor suggests. When the plate arrives, all else is forgotten; truly fresh fish, broiled just tender, takes an immediate grip upon one's attention. As the cool August evening turns to night, the bartender suggests blueberry cobbler for dessert. These small wild berries have lured people and bears down to the coast since time immemorial. A cobbler, the simplest form of cake and fruit, becomes a natural feast when made just right.

But even the hardiest explorers need sleep. Could a room be found, even in the crush of August? The last room available is Room 11. It's not fancy but the bed is firm, and the window keeps one surprise for the morning—the sunrise over the harbor.

STEAMED MUSSELS WITH GARLIC, WINE, AND PARSLEY

SERVES 6

4 pounds mussels in their shells
6 to 8 garlic cloves, minced
½ cup chopped Italian (flat-leaf) parsley

1 cup dry white wine
4 tablespoons unsalted butter, softened

Scrub mussels under cold running water and debeard. Discard any that are cracked or broken or that don't close when handled. In a heavy pot, heat the garlic and parsley in the wine and simmer about 3 minutes. Add the mussels, cover tightly, and steam about 5 minutes, until all shells open (discard any that do not). Remove the mussels and keep warm. Boil and reduce the liquid for a few minutes. Remove from heat and add the butter, stirring until it melts and the sauce thickens. Arrange the mussels in soup plates and pour the hot sauce over them.

BROILED BLUEFISH WITH GINGER LIME SAUCE

SERVES 6

Bluefish, also known as cape blues, run along the Maine coast in August. Don't confuse them with Boston bluefish, which are actually pollock. Bluefish are full flavored, oily fish, delicious when absolutely fresh. The fillets can be stored for two or three days after the fish are caught by dipping them in a solution of one part lemon juice to three parts water. Lightly salt and refrigerate the fillets face to face, skin side out.

6 bluefish fillets, 6 ounces each

Brush the fillets with butter, and season with salt and pepper. Place under a hot broiler about 5 inches from the heat for about 5 minutes, or until the flesh turns opaque. Serve immediately with Ginger Lime Sauce.

GINGER LIME SAUCE   (Makes 1 cup)

2 cloves garlic, minced
2-inch knob of fresh ginger, grated
2 tablespoons dry vermouth
2 tablespoons lime juice
1 tablespoon white wine vinegar
¼ cup dry white wine

½ teaspoon sugar
10 black peppercorns, crushed
½ teaspoon dry thyme leaves
2 tablespoons mild Dijon mustard
¼ cup sour cream

In a small nonreactive saucepan, combine first nine ingredients and simmer to reduce, about 10 minutes. Strain through a fine strainer, pressing firmly on the solids. Whisk in the mustard and sour cream.

BLUEBERRY COBBLER

SERVES 6

2½ quarts blueberries
⅓ cup quick-cooking tapioca (not instant)
¼ teaspoon cinnamon

½ cup sugar
1 ounce creme de cassis
Juice and zest of 1 lemon

Mix all together in a 13″ x 9″ x 2″ pan and let stand for 20 minutes. Bake at 350° for 20 minutes. Remove from oven and add topping. Increase oven temperature to 425°.

TOPPING

1⅓ cups cake flour
4 teaspoons baking powder
2½ tablespoons sugar
1 teaspoon salt

2 ounces cold unsalted butter
1 cup cream
2 ounces butter, melted, for brushing top
½ cup light brown sugar, for sprinkling

Mix dry ingredients, cut in butter, add cream, and mix with fingers to form a ball. Roll to baking-pan size and place over berry mixture, trimming edges as necessary. Brush crust with melted butter and sprinkle on brown sugar. Bake at 425° for 15 minutes, or until nicely browned—not too dark. Serve warm with vanilla ice cream, heavy cream, or a little whipped cream.

Roasted Eggplant and Tomato Salad with Aïoli

Broiled Swordfish with Black Olive Butter

Garlic Mashed Potatoes

Almond Cake with Cherry Sauce

Families
Gather
in
August

August is the zenith of our short but glorious summer. Time seems to stand still. While the rest of the country swelters, Maine's brilliant August sunlight is cut by dense shadows, cold water, and pleasantly cool evenings. The village is at its busiest. Inns are full, every mooring in the harbor is taken, and summer homes overflow with families and guests.

This is the month most often chosen to commemorate life's turning points—weddings, anniversaries, reunions—and the Inn is honored to share in these private gatherings, large and small. Picture throngs on the porch awaiting the bride and groom, the dining room resounding with boisterous toasts, our daughter Jeanne in bright pink bows and silver shoes, always the ready flower girl, a 50th wedding anniversary celebration around one flower-laden table in the Churchill Room. The biggest reunion in our history was for Castine's old Abbott High School. More than 110 graduates came for a sit-down dinner!

We're often asked how long the Inn has been in *our* family. Although we've owned it for only ten years, the Inn has benefited from the attention of several generations, for all of our parents have spent time and effort making it a success. Their contributions have made the work fun. The Inn has become a family place, and not just for us. Many families in town have worked at the Inn from one generation to the next. The truth is an inn of twenty rooms is a large and complex business. Maintenance and care for it run deep.

A great gathering deserves a special menu, and if the group is a large one, there is high drama in the kitchen. As waitresses load tray after tray of eggplant and tomato salad and head toward the dining room, the cooks are poised for action. Timing is critical, so that from the first guest served to the last, the food is hot and perfectly cooked. In a production line, one cook transfers a sizzling swordfish steak to a hot plate; another spoons on Black Olive Butter. A third cook adds the Garlic Mashed Potatoes, with a pinch of chopped parsley, and passes the plate to a waitress. Meals are plated as fast as waitresses can make their way through the dining room with loaded trays. While dinner plates are being cleared, the long butcher-block table is covered with rows of glass dessert plates, each one getting its pool of cherry sauce in turn. Next come wedges of a rich almond cake, dealt out like cards to each plate. A third pass down the table to add a dollop of softly whipped cream, and dessert is ready to join the party.

ROASTED EGGPLANT AND TOMATO SALAD WITH AIÖLI

SERVES 4

There are several steps to putting this composed salad together, but the flavors and textures of ripe tomato, roasted eggplant, vinaigrette, and creamy garlic more than justify the effort. It makes an impressive first course.

1 large eggplant, not peeled
Kosher salt
¼ cup olive oil

Juice of 1 lemon
1 teaspoon minced fresh thyme
1 teaspoon minced garlic

Slice eggplant into ½-inch-thick slices. Salt both sides and let stand in a colander for 45 minutes to leach out bitter juices. Rinse well and pat dry. Mix together the olive oil, lemon juice, thyme, and garlic and toss eggplant slices in the mixture. Brush a baking sheet very lightly with olive oil and place the slices on the sheet in a single layer. Cover tightly with aluminum foil and bake at 350° for 30 minutes or until tender. Cool. Remove from baking sheet with a spatula to a flat-bottomed container. (Layer if necessary, separating layers with waxed paper.) Pour any remaining olive oil mixture over the slices and refrigerate. May be prepared one day in advance.

3 large ripe tomatoes
1 cup balsamic vinaigrette (1 part vinegar, or about 1 ⅓ ounces, to 5 parts olive oil, or about 6⅔ ounces)

16 fresh, whole basil leaves

Slice the tomatoes into ½-inch-thick slices and cover with the vinaigrette. Add the basil leaves. Store, refrigerated, in a flat-bottomed container.

AIÖLI (Roast Garlic Mayonnaise)

6 large unpeeled garlic cloves
1 large egg yolk
1 teaspoon lemon juice

1 tablespoon water
½ cup olive oil

Toss garlic cloves lightly with olive oil. Place in a tightly covered baking dish and roast at 350° for about 30 minutes. Garlic should be completely soft but not burned. Slide the garlic cloves from their skins into a food processor and add the egg yolk, lemon juice, and water. Process and, with the machine running, add olive oil in a slow stream. Add water to thin to consistency of hollandaise sauce.

To serve: Arrange 3 or 4 tomato slices on a plate and top with 3 slices of eggplant. Garnish with a few whole basil leaves and season with salt and freshly ground pepper. Drizzle with the aiöli.

BROILED SWORDFISH WITH BLACK OLIVE BUTTER

SERVES 6

Swordfish has virtually no fat in it and therefore dries out very quickly if overcooked. It is delicious served quite rare.

6 swordfish steaks, 1 inch thick (6 to 7 ounces each)

Brush steaks with butter or oil and season with salt and pepper. Place 4 inches under a hot broiler for 2½ to 3 minutes per side, basting with butter when turned. Cook only until still slightly translucent and serve immediately with a spoonful of Black Olive Butter or Anchovy Butter.

BLACK OLIVE BUTTER

½ cup pitted oil-cured Moroccan olives
¾ cup unsalted butter, at room temperature

Place in food processor and purée.

ANCHOVY BUTTER

4 anchovy fillets
¾ cup unsalted butter, at room temperature

Juice of ½ lemon

Place in food processor and purée.

GARLIC MASHED POTATOES

SERVES 6

4 medium russet or Idaho potatoes, peeled
6 garlic cloves
½ cup warm milk

2 tablespoons butter
Salt and white pepper to taste

Cut potatoes into quarters and place in a saucepan with the garlic cloves and cold water to cover. Cook at a rapid simmer until the potatoes just slide off the tip of a sharp knife plunged halfway into them. Drain and pass through a food mill. Stir in warm milk and butter and season to taste with salt and white pepper.

Mashed potatoes may be made ahead of time and kept warm, covered. If they become too thick, add a little more warm milk just before serving.

ALMOND CAKE WITH CHERRY SAUCE

SERVES 8 TO 10

1¼ cups sugar
8 ounces almond paste
1¼ cups unsalted butter, at room
  temperature
½ teaspoon almond extract

1 tablespoon kirsch (optional)
6 large eggs, at room temperature
1 cup flour
1½ teaspoons baking powder
¼ teaspoon salt

In a mixer, cream sugar and almond paste. Add butter, almond extract, and kirsch and beat until light and fluffy. Beat in eggs one at a time. Mix the dry ingredients together in a separate bowl, then add them to the batter and mix just until blended. Butter a 9″ springform pan, line the bottom with a round of parchment paper, butter the paper, and dust the pan with flour. Turn the batter into the pan and bake at 325° for 1 to 1¼ hours. Serve on a pool of cherry sauce, and top with a saddle of softly whipped cream.

CHERRY SAUCE

¼ pound dried cherries
½ cup sugar

1½ cups water

Bring water and sugar to a boil. Add cherries and cook a few minutes, until cherries are plumped. Remove ⅓ of cherries, and purée the rest in the liquid. Return whole cherries to the sauce. Chill sauce before serving.

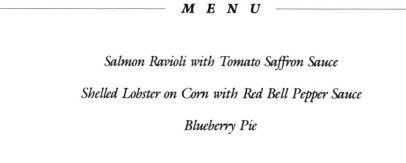

M E N U

Salmon Ravioli with Tomato Saffron Sauce

Shelled Lobster on Corn with Red Bell Pepper Sauce

Blueberry Pie

❖

Hurricane
Weather

❖

Beautiful as the end of August is, high winds can whip up leaves and toss flowers about wildly, signaling a seasonal change. Locals keep their ears to the radio, for every once in a while a real tropical hurricane winds its way up the coast from Florida. Harbormaster Ken Eaton and half the town drag boats on shore or sail them across the bay to the most protected coves. As the winds rise and the clouds boil, bedraggled sailors line up hopefully on the Inn porch to claim rooms left vacant by travelers encountering airport shutdowns.

Dinner preparations continue as we tape the windows, stow porch furniture, and check our supply of candles. Anticipation increases as the clouds darken, then explode with rain. Suddenly, no electricity, no lights. Without the din of the huge exhaust fan the kitchen is ominously quiet, except for the awful oaths of the cooks. How quickly we're thrown back to the nineteenth century without electricity, back to candles on the tables and oil lamps lighting the living room and bar. It gets hotter by the minute in the kitchen, where gas stoves and ovens are stacked high with bubbling pots and pans.

But we've never canceled dinner. We serve no matter what, because some stormbound traveler always needs a meal. As the dining room fills with grateful refugees, there's a sense of the fragility of life beside the powerful ocean. In the midst of the storm we tighten into the tiny isolated community that was simply a fact of life on the coast for centuries.

In the kitchen, normally easy jobs take extra effort. Biscuits require continual checking with a flashlight; without the electric dishwasher the human dishwasher is up to his ears in suds. Waitress duties multiply, yet every effort is appreciated threefold when a plate of salmon ravioli in tomato-saffron cream sauce appears out of the darkness. No one who tries this appetizer will forget the nugget of salmon mousse poached in its thin pocket of pasta. Next, under the flickering candle, comes a shelled lobster on a bed of fresh corn, laced with a mild red bell pepper sauce. Though the coffee machine is not working, one delicacy remains—a slice of blueberry pie. The fresh berries release their sweetness in a last, wild burst of summer.

$\mathscr{S}$ALMON RAVIOLI WITH TOMATO SAFFRON SAUCE

SERVES 8 AS A FIRST COURSE, 6 AS A MAIN COURSE

This recipe is time-consuming but if you like praise, this will bring it. The ravioli may be assembled a day ahead of time and stored, refrigerated, in a flat-bottomed pan in layers separated by waxed paper sprinkled with corn meal.

2 medium leeks, white part only, chopped and desanded
1 tablespoon unsalted butter
½ cup white wine
¾ cup heavy cream, not ultra-pasteurized
1 pound skinless salmon fillet, chopped fine
1½ tablespoons chopped fresh dill

¾ teaspoon salt
¼ teaspoon pepper
1 12-ounce package wonton wrappers (50 wrappers)
1 egg and ¼ cup milk, whisked together for egg wash
Chopped chives, for garnish

To desand leeks, chop them and drop in a bowl of cold water. Let the sand settle to the bottom; skim the leeks from the top. Sauté leeks in butter with a little water until soft. Add wine and reduce until nearly dry. Add cream and reduce by ⅓ to thicken. Cool the mixture, turn it out on a cutting board, and chop. Toss with salmon, dill, salt ,and pepper, and chop again to mix. The mixture should be a slightly textured paste.

Place 2 teaspoons of salmon mixture in the center of a wonton wrapper. Slightly moisten the wrapper around the filling with the egg wash. Cover with another wrapper, pressing down around the filling and from the center out to eliminate air bubbles. (Air bubbles cause "blowouts" during cooking!) Cut each ravioli into a round using a 3-inch cookie cutter. Pinch edges to remove any remaining bubbles and to seal.

Bring 8 quarts of water to boil in a large pot. Add half the ravioli (about 12) and cook 3 to 4 minutes, until the wrapper is cooked and the filling is warm. Remove with a slotted spoon and keep warm in the Tomato Saffron Sauce while cooking the other half.

Combine all ravioli in sauce, divide among warm plates, and garnish with chopped chives.

TOMATO SAFFRON SAUCE

If you can't get perfect tomatoes for this sauce, supplement the flavor with 2 tablespoons tomato paste.

4 shallots, minced
1½ tablespoons unsalted butter
1½ cups tomato, scalded, peeled, seeded, diced medium

⅜ teaspoon finely chopped saffron
1 cup heavy cream
⅓ cup dry vermouth
Salt and pepper to taste

Sauté shallots in butter until soft. Add the tomatoes and cook gently until nearly dry. Add the saffron. Add the liquids and reduce by ⅓. Season with salt and pepper.

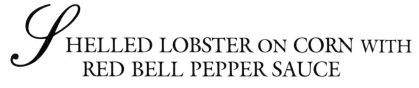

SHELLED LOBSTER ON CORN WITH
RED BELL PEPPER SAUCE

SERVES 6

6 lobsters, 1½ pounds each

To season water for boiling lobsters:
4 tablespoons black peppercorns
1 stalk celery, cut in chunks

Place the seasonings in 4 gallons of water and bring to a full boil. Plunge lobsters into the boiling water and cook for about 10 minutes or until barely cooked. (Hint: the antennae are easily pulled out at this point.) Remove lobsters from the water and cool. Reserve 2 quarts of the water.

9 ears corn
1 cup chicken stock
2 cups water
¼ pound unsalted butter

Shave kernels from the ears of corn and simmer in the stock and water for 20 minutes. Drain and toss with the butter, marjoram, salt, and pepper. Add sugar if the corn is not perfectly sweet.

Heat the 2 quarts reserved lobster water. Drop in lobster meat to reheat, 2 to 3 minutes.

1 large carrot, cut in pieces
1 onion
Seaweed (or substitute ½ cup salt if you don't have seaweed)

Shell the lobsters, taking care not to break the claw meat. Refrigerate until ready to use. This may all be done a day ahead of time.

1 tablespoon fresh marjoram
Salt and pepper
1 tablespoon sugar (optional)
Italian (flat-leaf) parsley, for garnish

Cover the center of a dinner plate with a thin layer of corn. Split the lobster tail lengthwise into two pieces and arrange along with the knuckle and claw meat over the bed of corn. Drizzle with about 2 tablespoons Red Bell Pepper Sauce and garnish with chopped Italian parsley.

RED BELL PEPPER SAUCE

1 red bell pepper
¼ cup chicken stock
¼ cup heavy cream
¼ cup white wine

1 teaspoon sugar
2 tablespoons unsalted butter, softened
1 tablespoon lemon juice
Salt and white pepper to taste

Char over an open flame or under the broiler, peel, and seed the pepper. Purée in a blender with the chicken stock. Transfer to a nonreactive saucepan; add the cream, wine, and sugar and simmer to reduce to ¾ cup. Stir in the butter until melted. Add the lemon juice and squeeze sauce through a fine sieve. Season with salt and white pepper.

BLUEBERRY PIE

SERVES 8

3 tablespoons cornstarch
⅛ teaspoon salt
1 scant cup sugar
½ teaspoon cinnamon

4 cups blueberries (1 quart)
1 tablespoon butter
Zest of ½ lemon
1 pre-baked 9″ pie shell

Mix all dry ingredients together well in a heavy-bottomed nonreactive saucepan. Add 1 cup blueberries and 1 cup water and cook, stirring, over medium heat until cornstarch is cooked and the mixture turns clear and thick. Add the butter, lemon zest, and the remaining 3 cups blueberries. Remove from heat. Fill the pie shell, chill, and serve with whipped cream.

Spicy Black Bean Soup

Roast Pork Loin with Apple Ginger Chutney

Braised Red Cabbage

Scalloped Potatoes

Baked Indian Pudding

The
Glory
of
September

❖

In late September, just as the first sparkle of frost forecasts the coming winter, Indian summer grants a luxurious reprieve. These few weeks of warm sun and frosty nights begin to tinge the tips of the oak and maple trees red-orange. Every minute spent in the sun is cherished. As young cooks, waitresses, and office workers return to school, the off-season travelers who prefer a more leisurely pace begin to arrive. We finally have time to sit down and chat with guests or enjoy an uninterrupted morning of gardening.

September also brings country fairs to celebrate the harvest. We wouldn't miss the Blue Hill Fair, two towns over. Teams of oxen pull a ton of granite blocks, their masters straining as hard as the animals, and the 4-H kids lounge in the straw with their prize goats. Every local Grange displays pyramids of canned goods and giant vegetables. Spinners and weavers bring out diaphanous skeins of colored yarns. Kids love the noisy rides and any game of chance, the sleazier the better. No "Corn on Cob" or "King of French Fries" can go unsampled. Above it all rises Blue Hill Mountain, serene and implacable.

An alternative is the Common Ground Country Fair, sponsored by the Maine Organic Farmers and Gardeners Association. Its exhibits of fine handcrafts, delicious food, and organically raised animals and vegetables are fun and instructive. Huge crowds show up every year from all over New England.

Cool weather calls for heartier meals, and our menus once again change to reflect the season. Robust soups, more meat and game, and fall vegetables begin to appear. A cup of spicy black bean soup just whets the appetite after a day outdoors. Thin, overlapping slices of juicy roast pork are garnished with a ginger-scented chutney made with local apples. Sweet and sour braised red cabbage offers the perfect foil for creamy scalloped potatoes. Indian summer would not be complete without one old New England dessert, Indian pudding, made from cornmeal and molasses and baked like a custard. We are as thankful for this simple treat as we are for the warm autumn sun.

SPICY BLACK BEAN SOUP

SERVES 6 TO 8

1 pound black beans (rinsed, picked over
    for pebbles, and soaked overnight)
1 onion, chopped
1 carrot, chopped
1 stalk celery, chopped
4 cloves garlic
2 tablespoons unsalted butter
1 cup ham scraps (ham, rind, ham bones,
    pork hock)

1 quart chicken stock
1 quart water
2 teaspoons ground cumin
4 teaspoons chili powder
Juice of 1 lemon
Salt and pepper to taste
Few dashes Tabasco sauce
Sour cream or lemon for garnish

In a large pot sauté the vegetables in butter until limp, adding the garlic for the last few minutes. Add the beans, ham scraps, stock, and water. Simmer for 2 hours, or until the beans are thoroughly tender. Add water if the level of cooking liquid falls below the surface of the beans, and stir often to prevent sticking. Add the cumin and chili powder. Remove half the beans, purée in a food processor and return the purée to the pot. Add the lemon juice. This should not be a thick soup, so dilute with hot stock or water if necessary. Season with salt and pepper and a few dashes of Tabasco. Garnish with a dollop of sour cream or a very thin slice of lemon.

ROAST PORK LOIN WITH APPLE GINGER CHUTNEY

SERVES 6

1 boneless center-cut pork loin, about
   3 pounds

For the marinade, combine in food processor:
5 teaspoons salt

2 cloves garlic
5 bay leaves, crushed
1 teaspoon leaf thyme
Zest of 2 lemons

Rub marinade into the entire surface of the roast. Place in a covered container and refrigerate overnight, turning two or three times before roasting, or marinate 6 hours at room temperature, turning three times. Remove meat from refrigerator 1 hour before roasting time to bring to room temperature.

Preheat oven to 350°. Scrape off excess marinade and roast the meat uncovered, fat side up, to an internal temperature of 160° to 165°, about 1 to 1½ hours.

Pour fat, if any, from the roasting pan and deglaze pan with a splash of water. This makes a nice juice to spoon over the sliced meat.

APPLE GINGER CHUTNEY   (Makes 1 quart)

2 pounds apples, peeled, cored, and sliced
   (A combination of cooking apples is
   best. Granny Smith and Golden
   Delicious are good and readily available,
   but Northern Spy are terrific if you can
   find them.)
½ cup dark brown sugar
5 ounces raisins
1 cup cider vinegar

1 ounce fresh ginger (a thumb-sized piece),
   peeled, minced
1½ teaspoons chili powder
1 tablespoon whole yellow mustard seed
1½ teaspoons salt
Zest and juice of 1 lemon
Zest and juice of 1 orange
⅛ teaspoon cayenne
¼ teaspoon cinnamon

Combine all ingredients in a heavy stainless steel pot and simmer until the apples are tender and flavors well blended. Keeps well refrigerated, or you may can it.

BRAISED RED CABBAGE

SERVES 6 TO 8

1 medium onion, chopped
1 tablespoon unsalted butter
1 medium head red cabbage, cored, sliced
  thin, and chopped

1 tablespoon caraway seeds
1 cup white wine
1 cup cider vinegar
1 cup dark brown sugar

Sauté the onion in butter in a heavy stainless steel pot. Add all remaining ingredients and simmer, covered, until cabbage is wilted and tender. Remove cover and continue cooking until most of the liquid has evaporated. Season with salt and pepper to taste.

SCALLOPED POTATOES

SERVES 6 TO 8

4 medium russet potatoes, about 2 pounds
2¾ cups heavy cream (not ultra-
    pasteurized)
1 teaspoon salt

¼ teaspoon white pepper
⅔ teaspoon freshly grated nutmeg
1 teaspoon minced garlic
1 clove garlic, cut in half

Peel potatoes and slice very thin. The slices need to be almost thin enough to see through, so it's best to use a mandoline or other mechanical slicer rather than a knife. In a bowl, mix the potato slices thoroughly with the cream. Separate the slices, if necessary, to allow the cream to coat each one. Mix in the salt and white pepper, nutmeg, and minced garlic.

Rub the interior of an 8″ x 8″ baking pan with a cut garlic clove. Butter the pan and fill with the potato mixture, which should be about 1½ inches deep when spread evenly. Add a little more cream, if necessary, to cover the potatoes. Bake at 250° for 1 hour; press the potatoes down into the liquid, and continue baking for up to another 1½ hours.

Note: As the potatoes cook, their starch is what thickens the cream in this recipe, so baking times may be somewhat shorter if you are using very starchy potatoes.

(Fresh potatoes are less starchy than potatoes that have been stored over the winter.)

BAKED INDIAN PUDDING

SERVES 6 TO 8

¾ cup milk
2 teaspoons white vinegar
2½ cups milk
½ cup yellow cornmeal
3 tablespoons molasses
½ cup dark brown sugar

5 tablespoons unsalted butter
¾ teaspoon ground ginger
¾ teaspoon cinnamon
½ teaspoon freshly ground nutmeg
½ teaspoon salt
2 large eggs

Sour ¾ cup milk by stirring in vinegar. Mix cornmeal with remaining 2½ cups milk until slushy. Heat, stirring occasionally, until thick like hot cereal, 15 to 20 minutes. Off heat, add molasses, brown sugar, and butter. Stir until butter melts. Add ginger, cinnamon, nutmeg, and salt. Stir well. Stir in well-beaten eggs and sour milk. Bake at 275° in a greased 8″ x 8″ pan for about 1 hour and 10 minutes, until set. Serve warm with softly whipped cream or vanilla ice cream.

MENU

Potato Leek Soup

Salmon Tart with Cream Cheese Crust

Tomato, Chopped Egg, and Basil Salad

Gingerbread with Rum Whipped Cream

❖

Head Table

Garden
Club
Luncheon

As the flow of summer travelers dwindles, year-round activities in Castine pick up again. In small Maine towns, governed by town meeting, much work is done by volunteers. Committees, boards, and clubs contribute tremendous efforts to basic town services. Every September Mark, Kathy, and Margaret don new caps—Budget Committee, School Board, Friends of the Library, and the Garden Club. The Inn hosts many town-related events.

The September meeting of the Garden Club at the Inn is a centerpiece of the fall season. First there's the orgy of flower arranging that shows off the end-of-the-summer garden at its best. Asters, sage, dahlias, and dusty miller glow in the center of each table. Branches of bright leaves, red berries, and rambling roses arch from tall vases. Every arrangement will be noticed by a close horticultural eye.

The ladies arrive in twos and threes, with sprightly step or moving more slowly. There is everything to be learned here about style and how to wear a hat. Along with their ready smiles, members bring a quiet commitment to preserving the town's character and tradition. And they're willing to act on that commitment, no matter what their age or physical condition.

Since the luncheon precedes the business meeting, speedy yet pleasant service is the order of the day. A steaming cup of potato leek soup gets the luncheon off to a warm start. No group pays more cheerful attention to the light texture of the biscuits that we serve with every meal. Conversation fills the dining room as everyone catches up on the summer and bids farewell to members headed south for the winter. A wedge of salmon tart with a delicate cream cheese crust is served cold, accompanied by a composed salad of late-season tomatoes with chopped egg and basil. Forks are soon poised for dessert—warm gingerbread with rum cream. Once at a potluck supper in Castine the entire dessert table was devoted to different gingerbreads from all the best cooks in town. Many of them are here. Let these smiling faces be our judge. A presidential fork clinks a glass, and quiet settles. Now you'll find out how things are done around here.

POTATO LEEK SOUP

SERVES 6 TO 8

6 leeks, white part only
4 slices bacon, diced
3 large russet or Idaho potatoes, peeled
   and sliced

2 cups chicken stock
2 cups water
Salt and pepper to taste
1 cup sour cream

Split leeks lengthwise, rinse well, and slice thin. Sauté bacon in a deep saucepan until most of the fat is rendered and the bacon is barely crisp. Add leeks and sauté until soft. Add potatoes, chicken stock, and water and simmer for about 45 minutes, or until the potatoes are very tender. Season with salt and pepper. Remove from heat and put through a food mill or food processor until smooth. Return to the saucepan and stir in sour cream. Reheat if necessary, but do not boil.

$\mathcal{S}$ALMON TART WITH CREAM CHEESE CRUST

SERVES 12

½ pound cream cheese
½ pound unsalted butter

Blend all ingredients with an electric mixer. Form into a ball, wrap, and chill overnight or at least 3 hours. Roll the dough, fit to an 11″ tart pan, and freeze. Line the frozen shell with aluminum foil, pressing the foil evenly all around. Fill about three-

2 pounds poached salmon (See page 36)
2 shallots, minced
1 tablespoon chopped fresh dill
2 tablespoons chopped parsley
⅔ cup sour cream

Mix together the salmon, shallots, dill, parsley, and sour cream. Season with salt and pepper and add a little more sour cream if mixture is too dry. Basically, what you're making here is salmon salad.

½ cup heavy cream
2½ cups flour

quarters full with dried beans and bake at 375° for about 15 minutes or until the edges are lightly colored and the bottom of the crust is set. Remove the foil (save the beans to use for this purpose again) and finish browning.

Salt and pepper to taste
½ large cucumber, peeled and sliced thin
Remoulade sauce (See page 36)
1 tomato, scalded, peeled, seeded, and diced

Fill the tart shell with the salmon mixture. Smooth the top and cover with overlapping slices of cucumber. Garnish each portion with a few pieces of chopped tomato and serve with remoulade sauce.

TOMATO, CHOPPED EGG, AND BASIL SALAD

SERVES 8 TO 10

This is a delicious, seasonal, composed salad that looks as good as it tastes. A couple of tips for this dish: If the tomatoes are less than fully ripe, just a few grains of sugar sprinkled on the slices will make them seem more ripe. Always snip basil leaves with sharp scissors. Chopping with a knife edge turns the basil dark.

3 large ripe tomatoes, sliced ¼-inch thick
15 large fresh basil leaves, snipped into
   julienne strips

2 hard-cooked eggs, chopped very fine

Arrange 2 or 3 tomato slices on each plate, overlapping the edges. Sprinkle with chopped egg and basil and drizzle with the vinaigrette.

BALSAMIC VINAIGRETTE   (Makes 2½ cups)

½ cup balsamic vinegar
2 cups olive oil
1 clove garlic, crushed

2 teaspoons Dijon mustard
Salt and pepper to taste

Whisk all ingredients together. Check again for salt and pepper before serving. Dressing will keep for weeks in the refrigerator, but remember to remove garlic after a few days.

GINGERBREAD WITH RUM CREAM

SERVES 10

4 cups flour, sifted
½ teaspoon salt
2 teaspoons baking soda
2 large eggs
1 cup sugar
1 cup squash purée (or pumpkin)
1 tablespoon grated fresh ginger

Butter a 12-cup Bundt pan and dust with flour.

Sift together flour, salt, and baking soda. Beat the eggs and sugar together and mix in the squash, fresh ginger, oil, molasses, and spices.

1 cup heavy cream
2 tablespoons dark rum

Whip the cream with the rum and sugar to soft peaks. Serve over the warm gingerbread.

1 cup vegetable oil
1 cup molasses
3 teaspoons ground ginger
2 teaspoons cinnamon
2 teaspoons cloves
1 teaspoon freshly ground nutmeg
1 cup boiling water

Mix in the boiling water (it is important that the water be boiling to activate the baking soda). Mix in the dry ingredients and pour into the prepared pan. Bake at 350° for about 50 minutes, or until a skewer inserted in the center comes out clean.

1 tablespoon sugar

M E N U

Winter Squash Soup with Blue Cheese and Toasted Walnuts

New England Boiled Dinner

Apple Pie

Homecoming

As the path of the sun moves farther south and golden leaves litter the streets, the Maine Maritime Academy, our neighbor at the top of Main Street, hosts its Homecoming Weekend. Since 1941 the Academy has been the training ground for young people who choose to follow Maine's seafaring tradition. From the early 1800s Mainers with the fortitude, the independence, and the love of the water to withstand this difficult life have traveled around the world and come back to name their Maine hometowns China, Belfast, Moscow, or Belgrade.

When graduates return for Homecoming, we see vividly how the tradition continues. Men and women come from jobs aboard commercial shipping vessels, on tugs and barges, in shipyards and boatyards, or in engineering and yacht-design firms to renew friendships and ties with the school. The Academy is leading the way in the highly technical training required for today's maritime workforce.

Homecoming Weekend is a good time to see the Academy's impressive fleet. Dominating the harbor is the *State of Maine*, the 570-foot training ship that hovers over the town. The research vessel *Argo* and the tugboat *Pentagoet*, along with yachts and sleek sailboats, are kept busy with tours and junkets around the bay. The pride of the fleet is the 87-foot wooden schooner *Bowdoin*, built for Admiral MacMillan's exploration of the Arctic.

When the football game is over, the sun's last, slanting rays follow the alumni back to the Inn for dinner. The rich autumn flavor of winter squash soup takes the chill off. Throughout New England, fall dining means boiled dinner—a medley of corned beef, cabbage, potatoes, carrots, beets, and turnips, served with horseradish. Each item must be cooked so that it retains its identity yet melds its flavor with all the others. The trick in preparing this dish is to keep it from becoming a stew. The plate itself is a joy to behold, with its fan of bright colors and shapes. There could be nothing better to crown this Homecoming meal than a slice of warm apple pie, a classic dessert when made with care and served with a wedge of cheddar cheese.

WINTER SQUASH SOUP WITH BLUE CHEESE AND TOASTED WALNUTS

1 medium onion, chopped
1 celery stalk, chopped
2 carrots, shredded
2 tablespoons unsalted butter
3 pounds acorn squash, peeled, seeded, cut into chunks
2 cans (13¾ ounces each) chicken stock, or equivalent homemade stock

¾ teaspoon freshly ground nutmeg
½ teaspoon salt
¼ teaspoon white pepper
1 cup heavy cream (not ultra-pasteurized)
Blue cheese and chopped, toasted walnuts for garnish

Sauté onion, celery, and carrots gently in butter. When soft, add the squash and the chicken stock. Bring to a simmer and cook until the squash is tender. Purée in batches in a blender; add seasonings and cream. If the soup is too thick, dilute to desired consistency with a little more hot chicken stock or water. Garnish with crumbled blue cheese and walnuts.

$\mathcal{N}$EW ENGLAND BOILED DINNER

SERVES 8

1 piece of corned beef brisket (or point
   cut), about 6 pounds
3 cloves of garlic, crushed

10 black peppercorns
2 bay leaves
6 whole cloves

Rinse the brine from the brisket and
place, fat side up, in a pot that will just
hold it. Add the garlic, peppercorns, bay
leaves, and cloves. Add cold water to cover,
and weight the meat so that it stays covered

(an enameled iron pot lid works well).
Simmer about 2 hours or until tender.
Remove the meat from the broth and keep
warm.

1 large head green cabbage
4 large potatoes, peeled and quartered
6 carrots, peeled and cut in sticks
1 rutabaga, peeled and cut in chunks

3 pounds beets, scrubbed
Horseradish, mustard, and vinegar as
   accompaniments

Remove tough outer leaves from the
cabbage. Slice into 8 wedges, leaving the
core intact. Simmer in the corned beef broth
for 15 to 20 minutes, or until tender but not
overcooked. Remove from the broth and
keep warm.

Put the potatoes, carrots, and rutabaga in the
broth and simmer until tender, about 20
minutes.

Meanwhile, boil the beets separately until
they just slide off the point of a paring knife

plunged halfway into them. (Beets are nearly
indestructible so don't worry about
overcooking them.) Cool them slightly and
rub with a cloth to remove the skins. Quarter
large beets; serve small beets whole.

To serve, slice the corned beef into thin slices
across the grain. Arrange the slices in the
center of a large platter and surround them
with the cabbage wedges and vegetables.
Spoon a little of the hot broth over the meat
to moisten it. Pass horseradish, mustard, and
vinegar separately.

APPLE PIE

SERVES 8

We like to use a combination of different kinds of apples in our pies. One of our favorites, though hard to find, is the Northern Spy. Other good cooking apples are Macintosh, Cortland, and Granny Smith.

½ cup shortening, chilled
¼ cup unsalted butter, chilled

1 teaspoon salt
2¼ cups flour

Measure shortening and butter into a bowl and sprinkle with the salt. Cut in flour. Add cold water until dough will just hold together (4 to 5 tablespoons). Divide into two balls and refrigerate.

4 or 5 apples (about 1 ½ pounds), peeled, cored, and sliced into irregular pieces
¾ cup sugar (more for tart apples)
¼ teaspoon freshly grated nutmeg
1 teaspoon cinnamon

1 tablespoon flour
1½ tablespoons butter
1 slightly beaten egg white
Sliced cheddar cheese or heavy cream

Mix apple slices with nutmeg, cinnamon, and flour and set aside.

Roll out one ball of pastry and fit into a 9″ pie plate. Fill with the apples and dot with the butter. Roll other ball for top crust and cut steam vents in it. Place over apples, trim, and crimp edges. Brush with slightly beaten egg white. Bake at 375° for about 45 minutes or until nicely browned.

Serve warm with a slice of cheddar cheese or a little heavy cream.

Mussel and Corn Chowder

Venison Steak with Game Sauce and Spaetzle

Broiled Tomato

Crème Brûlée

Hunter's Moon

❖

Darkness slips in earlier each evening, until one clear night what looks like a new planet rises out of the bay. Huge and pale red hovers the full moon of October, the Hunter's Moon. Many of the crew now head off to winter jobs. Bartenders become carpenters or school teachers, waitresses turn out Christmas wreaths, and innkeepers make repairs on their winter dens. Taking on a different job with each season is the traditional way of life in these parts.

Soon the winter shutdown of the Inn will begin in earnest. The porch furniture will be stacked in the darkened dining room again, the kitchen will get its end-of-season cleaning, and (last of all) the pipes will be drained and the water shut off. But the last few weeks before closing are a time to enjoy. Dinners become more communal as we reduce our hours and simplify the menu. The few of us left in the crew play all the bases, so visitors see familiar faces at every turn. The scattering of townspeople and a few hardy travelers are soon swapping stories. Often, one of us has time to join the party.

When the dark months come, the wildness of Maine seems much closer all around. The scent of game is in the air. Rabbit, pheasant, duck, and venison appear on our menu to appease the insistent growl of winter appetites. In the bar, now dark as a cave by 4:30 in the afternoon, a table can be pulled close to the fire for diners who want to enjoy some of the last and best tastes of the year. The mussel and corn chowder is a savory combination to ruminate over while talk turns to tracking, ice fishing, and snow. Just as the bright flames begin to mesmerize, in comes the platter of venison, the dark meat enhanced with a game sauce, circled with spaetzle, and set off with a red roasted tomato. Nothing more is heard except a whisper from far back in some smoky prehistoric cave, "It's good."

After a glass or two of dark red wine, and some tips on how to bait bear, our diners are ready for crème brûlée. Devotees of this fabled custard, called "burnt cream," have tracked it through all the culinary caves of Europe, where hunters raise their spoons with unerring aim (the French have a special spoon just for this delectable task). Breaking through the crust of hot burnt sugar, one dips into a cool, creamy custard. The combination of hot and brittle, cool and smooth never ceases to elevate the senses. And tiny flakes of vanilla bean await eager scraping from the bottom of the dish.

MUSSEL AND CORN CHOWDER

SERVES 8 AS AN APPETIZER,
6 AS A MAIN COURSE

2 pounds mussels in their shells
½ cup white wine
4 slices bacon, diced
1 medium onion, finely chopped
2 10-ounce boxes frozen corn, thawed, or
    the shaved kernels of 6 ears of fresh corn

2 cups heavy cream (not ultra-pasteurized)
Salt and pepper to taste
3 green onions, chopped

Scrub the mussels under cold running water and remove the beards. Discard any mussels that have cracked or broken shells or that do not close when handled. Pour the wine into a nonreactive saucepan, add the mussels, and steam them until they open, about 4 to 5 minutes. Transfer the mussels and the liquid to a bowl and let cool. Discard any mussels that have not opened. In the same saucepan, sauté the bacon until crisp. Remove the bacon from the pan and pour out all but 4 tablespoons fat. Add the diced onion and stew gently for 10 minutes. Remove the mussel meats from the shells and check again for cleanliness. Strain the liquid through several layers of cheesecloth into the saucepan. Add the cream, bacon, and mussel meats. Add the corn to the pot and simmer very gently for 20 minutes. Taste for salt and pepper and serve garnished with the chopped green onion.

VENISON STEAK WITH GAME SAUCE AND SPAETZLE

SERVES 8

By law we can serve only farm-raised venison. It is milder than wild venison and depends heavily on stock and sauce for flavor. If you have access to wild venison, so much the better.

For this recipe we bone a whole venison loin, saving the bones and scraps to make stock, and slice the meat into ¼-inch-thick medallions. A whole loin will serve 12 to 15. To serve 8, you should buy about 3 pounds of venison from your butcher and ask for 4 to 5 pounds of bones (substitute veal bones if you have to).

3 pounds venison
4 to 5 pounds venison bones, cracked with
  a cleaver
2 large onions
3 to 4 carrots, peeled
2 stalks celery
2 cups red wine

4 sprigs fresh French thyme
½ cup parsley stems
3 bay leaves
½ teaspoon peppercorns
20 juniper berries, bruised
6 garlic cloves, unpeeled
4 tablespoons butter, divided

Toss garlic cloves lightly with a small amount of olive oil. Roast for about 30 minutes in a tightly covered dish in a 350° oven. Set aside. Increase oven temperature to 450°.

Film a large roasting pan with oil. Add the bones and brown in oven to a dark nut-brown. The browning step determines the color and depth of the finished sauce. Cut coarsely the onions, carrots, and celery. Add them to the pan and continue roasting until they brown, stirring frequently. Be careful not to burn either the bones or vegetables, as the taste will come through in your sauce.

Transfer the bones and vegetables to a nonreactive stock pot. Deglaze the roasting pan with 2 cups red wine. Cover the bones and vegetables with cold water and the deglazing liquid. Add the thyme, parsley stems, bay leaves, peppercorns, and juniper berries. Bring to a simmer and cook for 4 to 6 hours. Skim periodically and replace liquid as necessary.

Strain the stock through a colander, discard the bones and vegetables, and return the strained liquid to the stockpot. Simmer to reduce by half, about 2 hours. Slide garlic cloves from their skins and add to stock during the last hour. Strain through a fine strainer.

Measure out 2½ cups of the stock and reserve the rest for another use (it freezes well).

Sauté the venison medallions in butter until rare to medium rare, about a minute on each side. Meanwhile, heat but do not boil the 2½ cups of stock. Add 2 tablespoons butter and stir until the butter just melts. Check for salt and pepper. (Optional: whisk in ¼ cup pureed Castine Inn Blueberry Jam.)

Arrange the medallions (3 to 4 per person) on warm plates and spoon the sauce over them.

SPAETZLE   (Serves 8)

3¾ cups all-purpose flour
¾ teaspoon salt
¼ teaspoon pepper
¼ teaspoon nutmeg

6 eggs
1 cup milk
1 cup heavy cream

Mix the flour with the seasonings in a large bowl. Beat the eggs with ½ cup milk until just mixed. Make a well in the flour and pour the egg mixture in. Work from the center to the sides, pulling the flour into the eggs. Gradually add the remaining liquids. Let stand for 20 minutes.

Force the dough through a spaetzle cutter or colander into boiling salted water. Boil until the noodles float, remove them, and place in ice water. Drain and toss with a little vegetable oil. The spaetzle may be made up to this point well in advance.

To serve, sauté in butter until lightly golden. Season with salt and pepper.

BROILED TOMATO

SERVES 8

4 large ripe tomatoes, halved
2 teaspoons fresh sweet basil, minced
2 cloves garlic, finely minced
2 tablespoons grated parmesan cheese

½ cup unseasoned bread crumbs
2 tablespoons butter
Salt and freshly ground pepper

Combine the basil, garlic, parmesan cheese, and bread crumbs. Sprinkle generously on the cut surfaces of the tomatoes. Dot with butter and season with salt and pepper. Bake at 350° for 10 to 15 minutes, until heated through but not mushy. Slip under the broiler briefly to brown.

CRÈME BRÛLÉE

SERVES 8

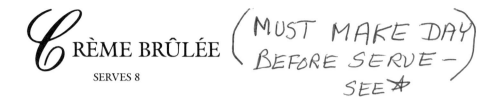

(handwritten: MUST MAKE DAY BEFORE SERVE — SEE ✷)

✷ Prepare this recipe a day in advance, as the custard must be completely chilled before you apply the sugar glaze.

1 quart heavy cream (not ultra-pasteurized)
1 vanilla bean, split and scraped
¾ cup plus 2 tablespoons sugar

Pinch salt
9 large egg yolks
1 cup light brown sugar

In a heavy saucepan heat cream with sugar, vanilla bean, vanilla scrapings, and salt just until sugar dissolves. Do not boil. Mix thoroughly but gently into egg yolks (don't whisk as it will introduce air bubbles). Allow mixture to steep for 20 minutes. Strain through a fine sieve. Place 8 shallow ovenproof dishes in a large sheet pan on your oven rack. Fill each dish with 6 ounces of the custard. Pour boiling water into the sheet pan up to the height of the custard in the dishes. Bake at 300° for about 30 minutes, or until just set. The custard should jiggle like jello when done; it will continue to set as it cools. Cool, then cover with plastic wrap and refrigerate.

For the topping: Spread light brown sugar on a baking pan and place in a 200° oven for several hours until dry. Push through a coarse strainer to remove all lumps.

To serve: Blot the surface of each custard with a paper towel to remove any moisture. Sprinkle sugar in a thin layer on top of each and shake off all that doesn't stick, leaving just a dusting. Broil until sugar melts and browns. (We use a propane torch from the hardware store instead of the broiler—it works great!)

FTERWORD

We hope you've enjoyed seeing the Inn from the inside out, following us through the seasons, tasting the flavors of our particular spot on the coast of Maine. The year 1994 is our tenth anniversary at the Castine Inn, and there could be no better way to celebrate the fruits of our labors than to share them with you.

INDEX

$\mathcal{I}$NDEX BY NAME OF RECIPE

"I only see ice," said the bear.
"How will I get to the fish?"
"Find a hole in the ice," said
the fox. "Put your tail in the hole.
Fish will come."

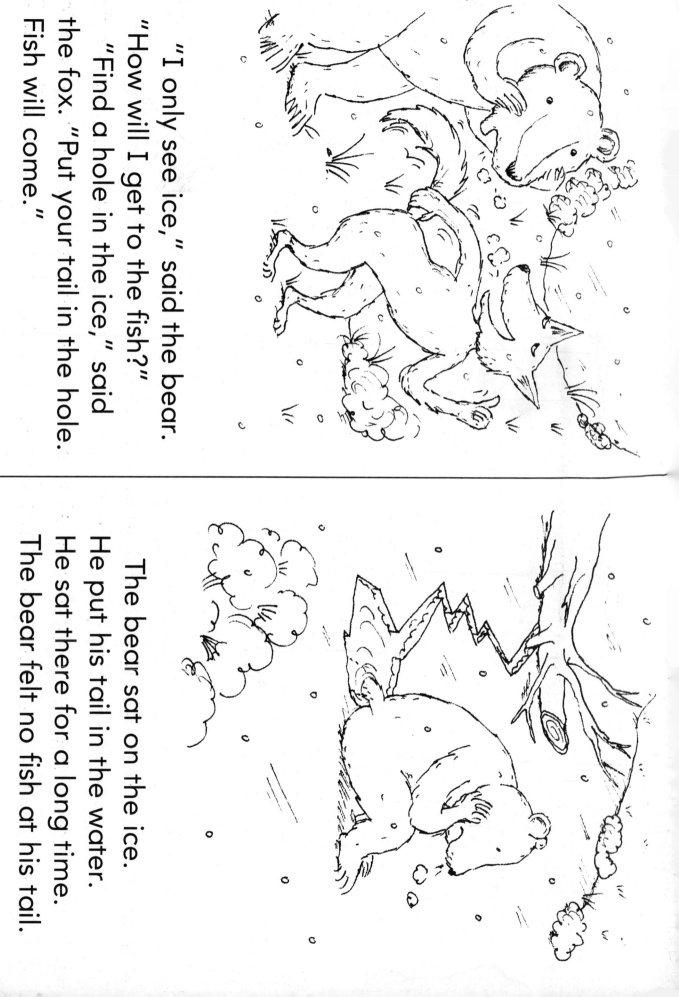

The bear sat on the ice.
He put his tail in the water.
He sat there for a long time.
The bear felt no fish at his tail.

"Fox," said the bear. "What
do you eat when it's so cold?"
The fox laughed. "I eat fish
from the water," he said.

②

Night came. The bear tried
to move. "The ice is holding
my tail!" he cried.
"This is no way to catch fish!
That fox has made fun of me!"

⑤